For Donna Louise Lupkin,
my first investor when she was broke,
my light when I failed,
my cheerleader when I won,
my reminder that life
is so much more than money.
Gone too soon.
Miss you.

"In oneself lies the whole world and if you know how to look and learn, the door is there, and the key is in your hand. Nobody on earth can give you either the key or the door to open, except yourself."

Jiddu Krishnamurti

Book reviews

"Ads and formulaic approaches can only go so far on social media, whereas meaningful relationships hold infinite possibilities. Jim Lupkin has artfully combined strategy and the human connection to create a system for social media success. Jim weaves intriguing stories, demonstrating the effectiveness of his philosophy, together with a clear cut, easy to digest system that you can effectively implement.

But what I enjoy most about Jim's system is the human side. By following the strategies outlined in Jim's book you will create deeper connections with a diverse network of individuals, and yes, it will lead to profitable results.

Most importantly this book will enrich your life. It delivers on a much deeper level than you might expect, offering you the opportunity to achieve life-changing results for your business and personal life."

Marla Tabaka
Leading Inc. magazine author and international success coach helping businesses reach as high as $45 million in revenue

"Why a Never Run Out of People to Talk to book? Because talking to real people, building relationships, and being normal is much better than creating conditional friendships, spamming generic prospects into funnels, and conducting our life as nothing more than a series of transactions. People notice. People smell insincerity. It is okay to have friends that are not business partners.

So, read this book. Learn how Jim Lupkin does this every day in business on social media."

Tom 'Big Al' Schreiter
Author of 30+ books on marketing

"I use the same principles as Jim Lupkin when I teach business owners how to grow their businesses via face-to-face networking. It's why I support Jim. Jim's mastered online what we all know works offline. What's unique about Jim is that he understands the value of that one connection and turning that connection into a relationship for anything productive to happen. My favorite piece, though, is how eloquently Jim explains the power of commonality. We all want to belong, and the easiest way is connecting with those that have similar interests.

It's easy to see why people trust Jim and why many businesses around the world use Jim's methodology. Jim shows you how to build a network of people that will become customers and tell their friends about your business. And that's how businesses grow!"

Gelie Akhenblit
Founder of the largest network of
business professionals in Arizona with
over 40,000 members

"From being one of the first distributors to do a million dollars in sales (8 million dollars today) to holding executive roles like Chairman of the Board for companies in the US and Asia to co-founding the oldest and largest association called SNA (formerly MLMIA), I've had an incredible 61 years. Social media has drastically changed what we do, and it can be for the better, as long as we have someone who can help us navigate this new territory. Social media can allow everyone to succeed faster than ever before.

After being full-time since 1957, I have never met anyone with more experience of how to use social media to grow a direct sales or network marketing business than Jim Lupkin. I believe this book, and Jim, will help my industry utilize social media the right way, to take us to a whole new level of professionalism."

Doris Wood
President Emeritus, SNA (MLMIA) and one of the most highly recognized authorities in the world on direct sales and network marketing

"After being in online publishing for more than 12 years, working with some of the top digital publications and brands in the world, I founded FabulousArizona.com and became a mentor to other inspiring female entrepreneurs. My business path has taught me the importance of social media for business.

In Never Run Out of People to Talk to, Jim Lupkin breaks down how to use social media in a way that is very clear and easy to understand for any business. Jim offers relatable examples from his own life over the past 25 years using social media that you can use to implement in your business. Jim's book is an excellent way to understand better how to leverage social media to elevate your brand and business."

Cynthia Sassi
Founder of FabulousArizona.com – an
popular online lifestyle publication

A Letter from Dr. Mikel Harry

Some of you might recognize my name as being associated with Six Sigma, a business management system designed to improve the profitability of corporations. As a matter of fact, we deployed Six Sigma throughout Allied Signal, Honeywell, GE, Ford, and DuPont corporations, just to name a few, with unbelievable success. The system encouraged business to run more effectively and efficiently. Put simply; Six Sigma reshaped the way industry executes its work on a daily basis.

To do that, we didn't really invent anything. With Six Sigma, we built on the work of others and innovated the proper sequence, timing, and process—essentially the same inspired philosophy that Jim Lupkin has embraced his entire professional career. He hasn't invented anything, but his innovation is far-reaching. His vision and principles have phenomenal implications.

As with Six Sigma, Jim understands the best way to craft those nuances in an orderly, progressive, and meaningful way so that the social part of your business has maximum impact.

Social media. In a nutshell, what is it? It's about people coming together to build on a product or service: the features, the benefits, the merits, the value associated with that product or services.

Jim Lupkin is an amazing man. He's a dear friend of mine and colleague, whom I consider an absolute genius in the field of social media. Get into his innovation, learn all you can about it, and you'll find you have the same reaction as me: Whoa! I wish this had been around when I started Six Sigma thirty years ago. Would have made my life a lot easier.

Just as with Six Sigma, generating breakthrough faster, quicker, more efficiently, and more effectively than would otherwise be possible is only the beginning of what you can accomplish. With Jim's system, you're well on your way.

Dr. Mikel J. Harry
Co-Creator/Six Sigma
March 2017

Special offer from Jim Lupkin

As you read this book, you'll understand the **WHAT** and **WHY**, along with some of the **HOW** I use social media to never run out of people to talk to for business.

You'll want to learn more when you're done reading this book. How?

Please visit jimlupkin.com and learn how you can gain access to my social media system for free while having an opportunity to be certified.

Here's what you'll learn.

A simple social media system that yields maximum success by understanding the importance of sequence, timing, and process. The social media system is distilled into four key components. I call them the Four Cs: community, conversation, connection, and communication. Together, these four create a simple but powerful social media system.

The proven social media system is designed to help you master social media's learning curve, experience breakthroughs in your business as you apply the insightful principles, and gain confidence that you will become certified in a proven system and join our nurturing community of respected and successful business leaders around the world. I am devoted to excellence in teaching, learning, and research by having only the most experienced faculty in social media to help grow your business.

The social media system is customized for quick learning. Includes overviews, instructions, social media examples, summaries, reviews, stimulating content that includes unprecedented access to the rich and varied experiences- and lessons- from some of the most successful business leaders of our time, and a series of videos, unlike any business training you've seen before. Filmed to capture the essence of one-on-one membership, our faculty videos will feel like time spent with an old friend.

From day one, your social media system includes two tiers of support: a talented, social media learning platform team dedicated to ensuring your learning experience is seamless and an ongoing, 24/7 support system in an active community where supplemental learning takes place in the form of hands-on, interactive sessions with our faculty.

Social media is ever-changing, and we're dedicated to helping you navigate new interfaces and leverage them for business success.

CONTENTS

6 | The Four Cs

- The untold social media story
- Refining the four cs over a quarter of a century
- The four cs timing, sequence and process
- Working the four cs together

1 | Introduction

On Burgers and John Coltrane

My empire rested on a flame-broiled, fast food burger.

An assembly line of burgers, actually— each one emblazoned with fake marks so that customers thought the frozen meat had made an authentic connection with a grill. A manager in a paper hat told me I wasn't smart enough to run the drive-thru window. Accurate enough, I hadn't mastered the complexities of "would you like fries with that?" as he had, but by eighteen, I was the CEO of my enterprise. Instead of Friday Night Lights, I made Friday night cold-calls out of the phone book. I had exhausted my mother's network of friends. I often approached people who pumped gas with a smile, shook hands, and asked them if they wanted more money in their pockets because fuel prices were on the rise. Most of the time, I was obnoxious in that rare, perfect storm of naiveté and optimism and youth.

It was small-town Pennsylvania, 1997. I took the fast-food job to know at least one meal a day was guaranteed, to have access to disposable food at shift's end, so my mom didn't have to ration canned meat and saltines. I wasn't above flipping burgers or draining oil from fry vats, but I could not feel complacent. One memorable dumpster haul- a woman in a BMW 5 series idled in the drive-thru lane. Despite the frigid temperatures, despite her third position in the queue, her window was down. Jazz music flurried from her stereo. Ebony hair twisted neatly atop her crown. Shiny rings adorned nearly every tapping finger on her steering wheel. We made eye contact.

She smiled. "Hey, son. Keep up the good work."

Her jubilant fingertips continued to play the steering wheel in time to the melody as if she alone was responsible for the trumpet notes lifting into the night. The movement, the lightness in her tone, radiated warmth. I set the trash bags on the ground at my feet.

"Miles Davis?" I asked.

"Coltrane. However, I'm impressed. Someone's done right by you." Her voice lingered on syllables the way the brass instrument improvised space inside the melody.

"My mom loves all types of music."

The woman nodded her head. Cars advanced ahead of her. She inched her luxury car forward, clearing a path to the dumpster.

I didn't move. The familiar stirring in my gut at first contact edged me closer to courage. She had her act together. I wanted the same.

"I have a business proposition for you," I said. "Ten minutes. All I need to change your life."

She propped the sleeve of her wool coat on the door. "That so?"

I gave her my hyper-speed pitch, three lines, maybe four, before I added, "I'm just working here until I build my empire."

Her laughter rose above the idling engines.

I handed her a business card from my uniform pocket then remembered my filthy hands, my job, my place. I apologized.

"I live two hours from here, son. In Philly."

"I'll drive to you."

"I just bet you would."

My manager's voice sounded through the kitchen's side door. I picked up the trash bags and completed my trek to the dumpster. On my way back inside, the woman waved.

The next day, my phone rang. A familiar, slow-talking voice over the phone said, "Is this the young man who's going to change my life?"

Not a jazz number goes by that I don't remember that encounter. The next day, I made the two-hour drive and signed her to my service, as well as a few of her friends. For a time, I believed success was mine— my confidence, my courage — the perfect storm of naiveté and optimism and youth. Years later, I learned that I owed my success to Miles Davis.

Talking to a stranger in a drive-thru is networking. Talking to a stranger in a drive-thru about Miles Davis then staying in touch on websites— as was the case back then, Yahoo Chat— is social media. The internet is a powerful business tool, unprecedented in scope and possibility, but it can also be a lonely place without authentic relationships.

Society and technology have changed

Many of us have cut our teeth in the business world believing two principles of success: word of mouth does not grow a business long-term, and paid advertising is the only way to build a business. While these tenets may have been correct at one time, they are part of an old-school establishment that does not include the vast social resources available today.

I call these two principles the suspender mentality: one is rarely seen without the other, they're mostly unnecessary, both are trying desperately to protect the bottom line, and anyone raised in the modern world of social media would instead become a viral meme for the wrong reason than to be caught wearing them.

To understand why change is so essential, snap on some suspenders. Go ahead. I'll wait. Just for fun, let's think through the launch of business the old-fashioned way.

First, you tell your friends and family and then ask them to tell their friends and family and so forth and so on. Perhaps give a little incentive to ensure that people talk about your business. Before you know it, you have your first customers. Now that you have customers who have generated income, you use that money you made to invest in things that will really get the customers rolling in—the kind of stuff that makes a business grow—because word of mouth doesn't grow business long-term.

My friend, Amanda, snapped her suspenders during her 15 years as an executive for a successful internet bank. One day over coffee, she told me how word of mouth worked great when the bank was in its infancy. However, eventually, even though her customer base was growing, she was no longer able to track customer referrals. As a result, she had invested in paid advertising intending to get in front of a lot more people and track the success of the ads.

Snap.

In fairness, maybe it was the caffeine. I thought I had misheard her. Amanda had just told me that word of mouth rocked her business, but since she wasn't able to track referrals and lacked the control features she needed to make sound decisions about the growth of the bank, she decided to dump money into a vat of uncertainty and hope something good foamed to the top. Why buy into ads when she already lacked an infrastructure for quantifying word of mouth?

You got it: suspenders. Pouring good money after bad.

Here's how each of the following types of businesses did the same based on my 25-year experience:

- Independent Contractors (sales reps, direct sales consultants, network marketing distributors, affiliates, authors, general contractors, electricians, plumbers, painters and solopreneurs that work from home):

Fishbowls, posting business cards on walls in retail establishments, advertising on placemats in restaurants, phone dialers, the same lead list in the hands of ten other contractors, car magnets, banner ads.

- Small Businesses (realtors, mortgage reps, insurance agents, dentists, chiropractors, accountants, hair salons, catering, cleaning services, website design and business consulting): newspaper ads, radio ads, flyers, attending networking events to mingle with other people you can sell to or partner with, pay per click ads.

- Brands or Companies (Fortune100, 500 and 1000 companies): Local and national TV commercials, sponsor large-scale events, throw your product in a big box store like Costco or Walmart, secure time slot on QVC, SEO organic and paid optimization.

All of these businesses have one thing in common. Over the last 20 years, businesses used the internet the same way:

- Optimize SEO (search engine optimization) for a website

- Drive people to the website using a pay-per-click campaign

- Drive people using banner ads and other marketing tactics

- Build landing pages to collect people's contact information for follow up

- Follow up using auto-responder email campaigns with incentivized information to entice people to buy at that moment or sometime down the road.

At one point in time, the above worked exceptionally well for businesses of all types and sizes. Direct sales companies like Avon and Tupperware, network marketing companies like Amway and Herbalife, real estate companies like Century 21 and Keller Williams, insurance companies like State Farm and Allstate, and companies like Walmart and Target thrived using these tactics. Some of these methods still work today, albeit with varying degrees of success. However, times have evolved. The way people use the internet has changed. To be successful, businesses and companies must use social media.

Today, many businesses spend money on paid advertising through social media sites but then resort back to wearing suspenders when it comes to word of mouth. They take the email addresses harvested from social media's paid advertising and run them through autoresponders.

Does it work? Sure. It's better than many of the things they have done over the last 20 years. Is it the best way with what is currently available to businesses around the world?

Absolutely not.

Paid advertising on social media has its place in business. Infused properly, alongside word of mouth in much the same way ads have co-existed with word of mouth for the past 20 years outside the internet, ads are effective. However, instead of using word of mouth exclusively in the start-up stage and then abandoning the strategy, imagine the power of word of mouth throughout the lifecycle of your business.

That is an entirely different kind of snap.

A non-suspender snap.

Paid advertising, by itself, is ruthless. There is no loyalty, no commitment, no compassion between people. Build a business around loyalty and relationships, and the trust fostered between people will help grow a company that will stand the test of time.

Social media allows word of mouth to grow a business long-term.

Together, let's bring an end to the old way of doing business. Let's pack away the suspenders and create a revolution where word of mouth has significance in your business.

Where relationships matter.

Where you succeed.

Where your customers succeed.

If you read no further, remember...

Today, if done correctly, social media builds the strongest relationships. We all want to be part of something bigger than ourselves. We want to talk with like-minded people. We want to be a part of a group of friends who know, like, and trust us.

In the internet age, social media means:

- Reaching out to make new connections online
- Having great conversations
- Continuing the valuable communication over time
- Building trusted relationships with the community you have inspired

Dynamic relationships are vital to a business's success and should be rewarded accordingly. Meaningful bonds present an opportunity to influence trusted relationships. Sharing passions and experiences at the right time strengthens the likelihood that friends will consider doing business with you.

The impact of social media

Social media has come a long way since 1995. Yes, it's been around that long, and some people would argue longer. To me, social media is about making new friends online then turning those new friendships into customers and referrals, something I have been doing since October 1995. Most people didn't gravitate towards social media in the 1990s because there weren't enough people accessing the internet to build relationships. However, the number of new people accessing the internet each year has resulted in an exponential increase in online relationships. In 1995, less than 1% of the world population had an internet connection. In 2019, 45% of the world population has internet access. The number of internet users increased tenfold from 1999 to 2018.

- First billion users in 2005
- Second billion in 2010
- Third billion in 2014
- Fourth billion in 2018

Out of the four billion internet users worldwide in 2018, approximately 3.4 billion are social media users. That means 85% of everyone who accesses the internet worldwide also is on social media!

In 1997, I went to a floral shop to purchase a dozen roses. A sign next to the cash register indicated that the flower shop had taken their business online. I asked the owner if she was having success with her online presence. She answered, "I'm trying it out. Not sure about this internet thing. Might be a fad." Today, most businesses can't function without internet access.

In the early 2000s, social media expanded beyond message boards, forums, and chat groups. Blogs and social networking sites, like Friendster, MySpace, and Facebook, became popular because of the opportunity for more in-depth interaction between people.

Since the mid-2000s, social media has exploded. Interaction between people evolved from merely knowing someone's name and having a text dialogue to sharing rich archives of photos, history, and emoticons. Thousands of sites popped up, allowing relationships with people based on shared interests to happen online.

You will benefit from reading this book

If you're an independent contractor, small business, brand or company that wants to use word of mouth to grow your business using social media, you'll benefit from reading this book.

You'll learn the proper timing, sequence, and process I used to build each of my businesses using social media successfully. Inside the pages of this book are just as many stories of failures as successes. Laugh at my slipups. Learn from my missteps. Some of these stories will inspire you to apply social media to your business today.

Remember though; by the time you read this book, your favorite social media platform may have changed how you use its website. Because of this, I will graze over how to use my social media system for any particular social media site and focus on giving you the knowledge and open your mind to a specific set of social media skills to set you on the path to your self-discovery.

I will show you how to use my social media system on the most popular social media sites through the use of compelling online videos after you read this book. I can continue to update these videos as social media sites change to keep up with the latest technology innovations.

Social media creates new solutions to old problems.

Classic questions when growing a business are:

How do you never run out of people to talk to?

How do you find the time to talk to people?

How do you stay in touch with people?

How do you inspire customers to refer others?

This book addresses these questions and more. You will have a specific path to lead you to breakthroughs at every turn.

Once you finished the book, here is what to expect

- Expect to expand your connections with an endless amount of people to talk to

- Expect to intensify conversations that will enrich your life in unexpected and transformative ways

- Expect to boost your formidable community of trusted relationships with people who will be open to hearing about your business

- Expect to strengthen your communication, creating repeat customers and referrals

- Expect theories that stand the test of time and evolve as social media evolves

- Expect support from me, every step of the way. Your journey doesn't end when you read this book's last paragraph. Reach out and connect with me and others in more than 100 US cities and 96 countries who already use my social media system for business by visiting www.jimlupkin.com.

Notes of hope

Every business can benefit from an in-depth knowledge of social media.

Entrepreneurs with the next great idea no longer need to tap investors for massive capital to get their products or service to the masses. Word of mouth costs less money.

Small business owners with limited advertising budgets can capitalize on the effectiveness of word of mouth and implement a structure to track referrals, not merely haphazardly hope that satisfied customers will tell their friends.

CEOs and other executives who may have spent a sizeable portion of the company's budget on advertising can finally realize better sales results needed to grow and compete by using word of mouth.

Creative types who rely on social branding to draw attention to art, books, music, photography, theater and all other endeavors that feed the soul can use word of mouth to sell their works and get noticed by influential people in their industry.

For solopreneurs who work from home, selling products and services via online business and operating on a limited-to-zero marketing budget, word of mouth is the most cost-effective way to share your passion. It's free.

Network marketing distributors or direct sales consultants who struggle to hit the desired income or who earn a full-time living but cannot seem to break through to the next level of achievement already have a word of mouth foundation in place for massive growth. Grow that foundation, and everyone on your team wins, financially.

I wrote this book because I've been where you are and know there is hope.

Before I was …

- endorsed by Dr. Mikel Harry, co-creator of the world-renowned Six Sigma

- a co-author for Network Marketing for Facebook, an Amazon #1 bestseller and available through 65 of the largest direct sales companies in the world

- featured on Entrepreneur on Fire podcast for How Facebook Can Be Amplified in Your business

- published in AdWeek for 5 Kinds of Facebook Posts that Drive 186% in Monthly Sales Growth

- published in Inc. magazine for 9 Networking Tips to Make Money on Facebook and Social Media Tips to Conquer the Competition

- published in Direct Selling News Magazine for The Wonder Kid of Social Media and Facebook: A New Era in Building Relationships

- a social media content creator for authors like Mary Christensen

- appointed Executive Director of the Social Networking Association (formerly MLMIA)

...before I created this innovation in social media you are reading about right now, I struggled.

At the beginning of my business career, peers and elders frowned upon me for building relationships with people online. I was told it was the wrong way to build a business. One guy laughed in my face. In hotel meetings, people turned their backs on me as being the young naïve kid who was trying to build a reputable business with a computer. In the 1990s, the struggle to embrace social-technological advances was real. No matter how much success I had with my first business, I was never as respected as others who built a business the "right" way.

Things didn't change much in my next business venture. I had more success using social media, yet those in business circles chastised me for not following rank and failing to align my practices with what had always worked previously. My self-worth usually took a monthly nosedive with the end of the month numbers.

Ever start a business on a pipe dream, with more passion than money? Me too. I had 30 days of capital left to pay my salary, the salaries of 18 developers and seven graphic designers, and almost no money to grow my business. Stress intensified because our employees had to make their wages to support families and obligations. Social media worked its magic, and we paid our team. Every month.

Above all, social media gave me hope. It is the one thing that has never let me down. Time and time again, social media has been the key that unlocked the business success I knew I was capable of. Social media can do the same for you.

How to read this book

Start at the beginning of this book. Don't jump around. Since the chapters build on each other, you have a specific path to lead you to breakthroughs at every turn.

Let's begin!

2 | Community

While in high school, I attended Pennsylvania Free Enterprise Week. The program is designed to offer kids an opportunity to see what it's like to run a business — picture two hundred business-minded kids, hungry to show off their enterprising skills. The camp was a Darwinian Shark Tank. Lord of the Flies in preppy ties and argyle socks. We bonded quickly as our seven-day survival plan depended upon us capitalizing on the strengths of each kid. Nicknames shaped our new identity. Mine was Rico. I want to say it was because I was possibly the suave one, that I conjured up a likeness to a baby-faced Ecuadorian-American rapper with far more hair, but I am at a loss to explain the name. Eight of us formed a go-to entrepreneurial mafia. Others asked us questions and sought help, and we reached decisions on behalf of the greater community. Fueled by ambition and enough high-fives between classes to rev our egos from zero to popular, the eight of us elevated our engagement, our drive, our focus that week, all because the environment fostered growth in the direction of success.

I also cannot say enough about what the Upward Bound program did for me in high school. Upward Bound provides summer learning opportunities for kids from low-income or low-opportunity families in a college campus setting. The program was a chance to get away from home, meet others our age, and have fun in an environment that set us up for success. The community atmosphere opened our minds to fresh possibilities. With positive, high-energy role models and mentors in place, we absorbed new skills and heightened our self-awareness. Outside of class, we bonded on the court over games of pick-up basketball and hung out in bookstores. In an environment where everyone strived to excel, even in the Friday-night skits, dreams took hold and possibilities ran wild.

I met Katie when I was a senior in high school. She attended a nearby school, and I went to prom with her. We were friends for just under a year before losing touch. Twenty-one years later, we found each other again on social media. We reestablished our friendship through a social media community and talked about our shared memories as part of the Upward Bound program. Katie promotes a product she believes in, and I had the opportunity to teach her social media.

It's always wonderful to watch people's expressions light up because they find friends forgotten over the years through social media communities. Life may have pulled them in different directions from their friends, but social media can be the great unifier.

Communities, such as those I experienced at Free Enterprise Week and Upward Bound, are abundant in local areas. However, there is a new horizon of the community at your fingertips, ready to open individuals up to the kind of success that unity brings. Virtual spaces like social media extend far beyond places you can reach by car. Imagine finding a strong core of like-minded individuals—not just those you can high-five in a hallway but those who can challenge your cultural perceptions and specialized talents—from countries all over the world. Also, think about taking all your local communities online through social media. Talk about dreams and possibilities running wild!

A community works on social media

The first C to mastering my social media system is a community.

Most people want to belong to a group of individuals who share common interests. That sense of belonging that the community brings to our lives helps us thrive. Unity drives us to do our best, be our best, and encourage the best in others.

Communities create an environment where people are more likely to do business with you and are more likely to stay in business with you for a more extended time. When everyone can be part of a community and join in from their mobile phone, this happens even more quickly.

Think about the last 30 people you asked to look at your business. Were you trying to move these people forward all by yourself, or did you introduce these people to a thriving online community filled with others who were already excited about your business? Don't go it alone. Let your flourishing community inspire people.

Your personal life

My father is a martial arts expert of more than 35 years. He had always wanted to learn Dim Mak, literally translated— death touch. Because Dim Mak is a rare specialty in the martial arts world, I suggested my father check social media out for Dim Mak experts. Within weeks, he had engaged in active communities with experts trained in the Dim Mak discipline throughout the world, something he wouldn't have been able to do without the power of social media. He is a real social media convert, all because he found a community of like-minded, passionate individuals who shared his interest.

Think about your product or service. Do you think there are people, like my father, who are curious to learn about a product or service like yours? Why not connect all these people in a community, talking about what you do and discussing your business and your industry at large?

Your business life

Your business community is like Free Enterprise Week, Upward Bound and Dim Mak. It's feasting on mutually-adored content for your business and elevating those around you to do the same. When people have commonalities around your product or service, they look forward to talking with each other regularly. They learn new things. People with shared interests are attuned to what others in the community say because of those uniting values. Also, communities of people often generate new ideas that take those commonalities in fresh directions for your business.

Communities are also about respect. Everyone in the community feels like a family. Participants are open with the community in a way they may not be accessible with others. Relationships formed out of similar likes and values around your business mission resemble sibling and best friend connections.

A community is one big group of people assisting each other towards a common goal. Business soars at a much faster rate in a community as compared to an isolated environment like email.

Inspiring your community

What do people think about you, your products or services, and your business? A community allows you to be part of that thinking process.

Maggie has been an entrepreneur for more than 20 years. She shares products that have made a difference in her life. She's a mom, speaker, and coach. Her passion centers around inspiring others to have their breakthroughs in life. She loves to travel the world and spend quality time with her three children.

Though Maggie had realized a modest amount of success in her business, she began to feel chained to the traditional ways of spreading the word about her products. The conventional methods pulled her further from her goals of travel and family time. Over time, the freedom the business promised was no longer delivering on that freedom. Maggie was resistant to changing the status quo because the old methods had brought her success, but she was burned out. That level of desperation became an opportunity to reimagine freedom with the help of social media.

Maggie didn't just dip her toes into the social media waters. Maggie dove in, head first. She brought her embrace-life mentality to building a community through social media a few years ago. Now, in less than 36 months, her business does just over $40 million a year in sales. She has more than 350,000 people in her community on social media, learning about her products and ways to refer her products to others. She sees consistent growth every month because she created an environment where people can learn at their own pace if her products will help them.

Here are four must-have ingredients Maggie and I realized were necessary to building a strong community on social media.

Frustration and Ask Questions

Before social media, easing your customers' frustration in real-time was impossible. Today, not only can you reduce it in real time, but you can be proactive and ease discontent before it occurs. Many frustrations go unnoticed because people do not want to call the business to complain about something regarding a product or service. These people usually stop ordering the product or service and purchase from a competitor. Many times, the frustration is user error and has nothing to do with the product or service.

Allow people to voice frustration and ask questions, giving you control over the narrative of your product or service. Addressing others when frustration is running high is one of the most exceptional services you can offer to your customers and those referring your business to others. Give those who do business with you a safe place to ask questions and honestly express themselves. You will establish a nurturing environment and become a sounding board for those who do business with you.

Picture that ideal environment: maybe a thousand or more people. At any given time, if something is bothering them, they can come into your group and ask any question, fully knowing that you and your business will do whatever it takes to serve them. Make sure they understand that they're free to voice concerns and questions and remind them of this freedom from time to time. The result is great loyalty to your business and a nearly unshakable social proof.

When you see a frustration post, post a comment to put that person at ease. Share your experiences with the product or service or business. Be specific and encouraging. You can make a difference in that person's experience. You would want that person to feel the support that can only come from people who have had similar experiences.

A day will come when someone will grow frustrated about your business. No one is immune. Your community is not the place to vent. It's easy for posts to be misinterpreted, to sound like someone is complaining about the business, when, in fact, someone is merely looking for answers.

Here are thoughts and examples of how to inspire others in your community.

After every post, you draft, take a breath, fill your coffee cup, stretch your legs, come back to the screen, then read the post aloud. Ask yourself: Does this post sound like I am complaining? How can I edit the post to retain honesty but stay positive? How can I edit the post to be perceived as someone seeking answers?

Here are examples:

> Honest and negative: I bought this product a few months ago, and it's not working. I'm frustrated.

> Honest and positive: I bought this product a few months ago, and I do not yet see results. I know it works. Can someone help me figure out what I am doing wrong?

> Honest and negative: I have been referring this product over a year now, and I still am not making money. Everyone tells me no. I wish the company had better tools than what's currently available.

> Honest and positive: I have been referring this product for over a year now, and I still am not making money. I know this works. Can someone help me figure out what I am doing wrong?

Subtle changes, to be sure. I'm asking you to own responsibility for your success as a customer or someone who refers. Full responsibility makes it easy, to be honest,

and positive instead of honest and negative.
Why? Because most people do not want to
talk negatively about themselves. They want
to find a solution and move forward.

If you're honest and positive inside the
community, then you can create positive
social proof while learning and growing.
Negativity breeds detrimental social proof.

Ethics and Lifting Others

When building a strong community on
social media, ethics and lifting others is
paramount. Love yourself and love others.
Treat people the way you want to be treated.
After all, they joined your community
because they believe in your business. If you
serve them well, they will be excited to tell
their friends about your product or service.
As a result of this nurturing, your business
will flourish.

Be that inspiration for your community.
Encourage. Lift. Tap into the power of
people all working together toward a
common good. Champion your business
family. Root for them. Elevate them.

Igniting community with social proof

The catalyst of community is social proof.

What is the difference between a few and many people joining your community?

Social Proof.

Second only to understanding the numbers, social proof is the most powerful thing I have learned over my two decades in business.

Suppose you drive past a seafood restaurant during open hours and the parking lot is empty. You assume the fish isn't fresh, the service is poor, or the atmosphere is dated or unclean. Conversely, you drive past a custard shop. The line at the window is twenty people thick, and the drive-thru line wraps around the building. You assume the custard is spectacular. Why else would people be willing to take extra time out of their busy day for this particular custard stand? Some call this following the crowd. Business-oriented people know this phenomenon as social proof.

Let's look at it from an old school meets new school business story.

Wayne was a bit old-school when it came to business. His idea of generating new potential business was setting up meetings at coffee shops. Wayne had a social media presence, but his sales team was stuck at $30,000 per month in sales. He needed social proof to take his team to the next level.

Wayne discussed several individuals he thought had the potential to be customers and refer his business to others. Cindy had a careful personality. Tempted by the product results she had read about and witnessed from others, she needed a nudge in the direction of opportunity. Ken was a social guy who was active on social media. He often posted photos of adventures with friends in his health-oriented lifestyle. And Molly was a nurturer, always taking care of those around her. Wayne set up a community on social media. Carefully and deliberately, the community swelled to thousands of members—far beyond Cindy, Ken, and Molly. Instead of Cindy staying in her comfort zone, instead of Wayne trying to convince Ken about the merits of his health supplement, instead of Molly deciding based upon isolated results from Wayne, the social proof Wayne built with his community moved Cindy and Ken and Molly toward a favorable decision. In a few short months, Wayne and his team increased sales to $60,000 a month.

Because of social media, social proof is the new marketing rock star method, far and above a few friends telling their friends over meetings at coffee shops.

Social proof can also destroy a business. Instead of others talking in favor of your product or service, they may complain because the product or service is not as great as you led people to believe. Now, instead of hundreds or thousands of people raving about your products and services, the negative buzz crashes your momentum. You'll be quickly out of business.

There are five types of social proof: Expert, Celebrity, User, Wisdom of Crowds and Friends. Some are more impactful than others; however, the Wisdom of Friends is the most important kind of social proof.

Expert

A credible expert or authority in your industry speaks highly about your product or service. If a dermatologist in the skincare industry mentions the benefits of your products, virtually an endorsement, you will likely to see an increase in sales from anyone who trusts that doctor. Find these experts on social media and send them a sample of your product or more information about your service to review. Get them excited. Add them to your community. Let others in the community see this credible expert and hear their passion about your business in the community.

Celebrity

An excellent example of a celebrity social media teaser campaign is Snapchat celebrity Shaun McBride, better known as Shonduras, who has compiled hundreds of thousands of followers. McBride was part of an ad campaign promoting Taco Bell's Cap'n Crunch Berry Delights. As part of the campaign, Taco Bell allowed McBride to take over its Snapchat account. His followers were notified that they could watch his grocery shopping experience via a video. He picked up a box of Cap'n Crunch and then he was transported into the Taco Bell's headquarters and went on to promote the launch of Cap'n Crunch Berry Delights.

Taco Bell continued to engage McBride in its Super Bowl 50 campaign. Taco Bell ran a Snapchat story to market the launch of the Quesalupa and people were encouraged on Taco Bell's website to pre-order the Quesalupa. The campaign resulted in 40,000 pre-orders.

Maybe you don't have the budget to hire a celebrity like Shaun McBride. What about a local personality? Let her fall in love with your product or service and then add her to your community on social media.

User

Think testimonials. A customer is happy with your product or service and puts forth a testimony in the form of text, picture, or video. These can then be shared in your community on social media.

How many people already love your product or service? Hundreds, thousands, more? Even if you're just getting started in your business, you might have ten testimonials. Share them. Even with a small community of 100 people, ten stories will move them to try your product or service.

Wisdom of the crowd

This kind of social proof speaks to the popularity of a product or service. Each time we see the term "most popular," our socialized brains want to know more about that product or service. We want to be in the know because it makes us feel informed.

When you post in your community on social media, the wisdom of the crowd can is measured by the number of likes and comments. High engagement tells new people considering doing business with you that this is a wonderful business. Don't try to build your business by yourself. Work with others.

Wisdom of friends

The most meaningful kind of social proof, the wisdom of friends phenomenon is when a friend tells another friend about an experience they had with a product or service they cherish. In turn, this passion inspires their friends to want to try the product or service.

Nothing is better than hearing about a product or service from a friend. The relationship is already in place. Inspire your customers to share your product or service with their friends and then invite these friends into your community.

When the social proof is applied correctly, odds of success increase exponentially. Never underestimate the power of a community raving to the world about your products and services. More people talking about your business translates to more momentum for your business.

Community Tips

Here are some tips for growing your business from the first C - Community of the social media system.

Social media allows you to build a community of people around your business. It's the primary reason it's possible to use social media as an addition to live events.

Enjoy these nine proven ways to create stronger communities with new people who will get excited about your business in a shorter period and keeps people excited about your business long after they start doing business with you.

Types of communities

Understanding the different types of communities helps you better serve those who show interest in your business. A customer group unites those who express interest in becoming a customer with those who are already customers. A referral group is designed specifically for those who wish to take your product or service to the next level of involvement and those who have already met with success as someone who refers your products or services to friends.

Potential customers

Do you have people who have expressed interest in becoming a customer for your business? Why convince them to try your product or service alone when you can have a group of excited customers doing the work for you? Social proof from others validates that what you're saying is true. A customer community unites those who express interest in becoming a customer with those who are already customers.

Existing customers

If you want to keep customers for a long time, provide exceptional customer service. It is very difficult—nearly impossible—to service all of your customers in real time without using a community on social media. People stay customers longer when they are in a community with other people who have the same interests and reasons why they're using your product. Building a culture around your business creates a movement. Even if a competitor undercuts you slightly, your customers will stay committed to you because they're part of something bigger than themselves, not just buying a product or service.

Potential referrals

As in the customer community, why do all the work yourself? Your community, filled with happy and energetic people who are referring your business to others, can inspire others who might want to refer your company. Let's change their lives more quickly than what you can accomplish alone. Hearing buzz about potential success can be a strong influence but witnessing and becoming part of that social proof is powerful.

Existing referrals

Just like the customer community, making sure the people who are already referring your business to others are supported is crucial to the long-term success of your business. These are the people who will sustain your business for years to come. Invest time to ensure they have everything they need to catapult their growth.

Types of Community posts

Make sure to create the right culture by knowing four types of posts that people enjoy interacting with inside of your community.

Ask questions

Asking questions allows you to keep moving forward with excitement and will enable others with the same issue who might be too shy to ask also to move forward when they see the answer. This is called proactive customer service. For the introverted in the community or those who don't yet have a question, question posts educate proactively. Members see answers to questions that they may have some time soon. Instead of getting frustrated, they will already know the answer to the question.

When you see others asking a question, and you know the answer, don't hesitate to respond. Show others that you believe in the product or service and are part of the community.

Share testimonials

Sharing testimonials motivates others that have yet to see the impact of the product or service and business in their own lives. It shows other people that the future is bright. It also holds you accountable to your new community of new friends and gives you that personal feel-good notion, knowing that the product or service or business is making a difference in your life and you're telling the world about it. It validates that you made the right decision.

When someone shares a testimonial comment, congratulate them on their success. Say something meaningful. Remember, you are part of a community that supports each other.

Share tips

Sharing tips help other members of the community get the most out of business. Others will start to share their tips, thus creating an even more significant impact for the product or service or business.

When someone shares a tip, be sure to comment and share a tip, as well. New tips or reinforcements of old tips, the impact and comradery are the same.

Updates

Giving an update on how the product or service or business is making a difference in your life is similar to a testimonial except you're provided the update based continuously on an experience you just encountered.

When someone shares an update, comment by adding more value to what that person said. It might be as simple as responding, I love your update! or That sounds like a great update. Here's mine. Again, it's all about building the community.

Frequency

Frequency plays a vital role, so communities are active and thriving. Without frequency, your communities can look and feel like a graveyard: silent, quiet, no signs of a pulse. People will wonder if your business is as good as you profess. If no one else is talking about your business, how great can the business be?

Frequency is important on both the administrator and member sides of the communities.

Administrator frequency

An administrator is someone who creates the community or is added later as a community leader after first being a member. Some administrators have full rights to add and remove people, or the communities might be structured to give certain administrators limited responsibilities, such as approving posts. No matter how an administrator assumes a leadership position, the community's success is a critical responsibility of the administrator.

As an administrator to the community, post daily. Consistent, fresh content in the community ensures that new people feel the group is flourishing. One idea for fresh content when selling a product is an ingredient series. Every week, you highlighted one ingredient and expanded whatever credible information you could find on that ingredient: the latest scientific research, royalty-free molecular-level photographs or images that conjured the desired results, maps in nature where the ingredient could be found, a bullet list of benefits for the body. Ingredient educational posts accomplished two things: they gave you fresh and organic content to post about your business, and they elevated knowledge on the product so that your team comes from an informed place when asked questions.

Robust interaction suggests success and has a tremendous impact on people deciding if they want to do business with you. If a potential customer visits a group on Thursday and the last time someone posted was Monday, the community will feel like a graveyard. That potential customer will hear mental crickets. If a product or business is fantastic, people should be talking about it frequently. An administrator can make sure this happens by posting daily content that gets people engaging.

Member frequency

A member is someone who joins a community but has no administrative control over the group. While the administrators lead the community, the members are the reason for the community's existence. Members can add other members, post in the community, and interact with other members posts, but they also serve an even greater purpose. Members engage in spirited discussions, have common interests, and support each other in their endeavors.

If you are passionate about the community's purpose, posting to the community three times a week keeps engagement and energy high. Administrators posting and members engaging on these posts are not enough to sustain a successful level of enthusiasm. Members must insert fresh content. People need to connect, bond, and build community. This happens when everyone is posting in the community and sharing stories. The more posts a new person sees, the more that person will believe in the business and want to experience it, first-hand. This contagious, energetic, emotional Velcro is the magic of social proof.

Privacy

On most social media sites, your community is open for everyone to see, even if they are not in your community. Keeping it open works best if you create a community for only customers and those thinking about purchasing your product or service. Your goal is for everybody to know about your product or service. Why block them from seeing anything?

On other social media sites, you can keep your community private to only those who are in the community. This option works well when building a community for those who are referring friends to your business or where you will provide specialized or high-end support if you have a group of premium or pay-extra customers.

You can also build communities that no one can find. Each member has to be personally invited by another member of the community. Are these communities used much? It's impossible to tell because you cannot find these communities or confirm their existence on social media unless you are personally invited. This option is not for customers because you want your customer interaction to be public. However, you may come across a unique scenario where a select group of silent business partners or team members need a private space to discuss matters of a sensitive nature.

Management

Allow members to add their friends, but administrators of the community must approve each new member. If you don't allow this freedom, then you are solely responsible for the community's growth, which can be a severe burden for anyone— me, included. Let everyone grow the community, together. As a result, social proof will come faster.

Allow members to post content, but you have to approve the posts. This gives you added protection to stop unsavory posts from going out to the community. This is the best way to prevent negative social proof from undermining your business.

Make sure that opportunities to add pictures or videos to posts in your community represent the community's purpose. If your community is focused on customers, then the images and videos should describe your products and services. If your community is for those who refer your business to others, then the pictures and videos should capture, visually, why customers would want to refer your company to friends.

For urgent messages you want your community to read, be sure to include images or videos, as these additions make the words more noticeable than text-only.

Always be notified when others post in the community, so you don't miss critical information for your business. Notification is a smart feature to turn on.

Support members in the groups

When you are referring the business to friends, the power of the community can be heady. Intoxicating. The dynamic of people working together to create something larger than themselves is a self-affirming high, no matter the objective.

Traditional influencer marketing keeps the power locked away inside individuals. Someone with a large following on a social media site must be dynamic and engaging and on all the time or his followers slip away. If a traditional influencer posts about a product that helped her lose weight, the product's company is likely to see a bump in sales. Traditional influencers feed the beast of what their followers want to retain them. Not everyone has the personality, dedication, or the stamina to sustain influencer status alone.

In contrast, the community unleashes the power of a team. Instead of one influencer being the lynchpin to success, power is distributed among all people in the business, resulting in an even more significant influence for everyone involved. Because of this community factor, trust must be high. Everyone in the community must support each other. A community can't thrive if members are looking out for their self-interests.

Community topics

Your profile on any social media site is the place to post about your own life. Being a member of a community is about discussing topics that relate to the purpose of that community. Your laser-like focus in community posts helps to keep the energy surrounding the product or service, which, in turn, benefits all and brings out the best version of you.

Introduce friends

When you're ready to add a friend into a community, it's crucial you introduce your friend to the rest of the members and tell them where to go in the community so that your friend can learn about your business.

You want your friend to meet others in the community and experience the power of social proof. If you do not introduce your friends to the community, members of the community have no idea that they should be connecting with your friends.

Community interaction

People interacting with each other in your community is crucial for your success. The best of business—the spirited challenges, the sharing of information, the friendly support, the culture of like-minded individuals—can be found in numbers. People interacting with each other.

A community of like-minded individuals shares an interest in a product or service. Different experience levels, specialties, and regions offer a unique and often global opportunity for enhanced knowledge and support.

As you visit your communities, you'll want to like and comment on other people's posts. A good rule of thumb is to comment when you have something meaningful to say and like or use one of the other emotions like love when you liked the post, but you're just not sure what you want to say about it.

3 | Conversation

Julian is a multi-billionaire.

I met him through a mutual friend whom I stayed in touch with through social media. He's taken twelve of his companies to a billion in sales. When I met him, I wasn't as impressed as I might have been because life had just dealt me a blow.

My mom came close to dying. At sixty-five pounds, in a medically-induced coma, machines ate and breathed for her. I paced the hospital wing, acquainting myself with the reality of losing my best friend. The vulnerability I carried with me into my meeting with Julian made me a bit reckless, fearless, honest in a way that only the reminder of impending death can.

Our 30-minute phone conversation had turned into a two-and-a-half-hour question and answer session about my social media expertise. Julian kept asking questions until he said, "How soon can you get here?"

I thought of my mom. If she knew a guy like Julian wanted to talk to her son, she would tell me to go.

"Day after tomorrow," I said.

Working with a billionaire was a dream come true. I had realized my echelon of success—at the time, hundreds of millions in sales for my clients—but I still believed that to change the world, one needed the kind of gravity that only wealth brings.

Two hours into a scheduled two-hour meeting, Julian asked, "Jim, what do you think about network marketing?"

Old Jim might have sugar-coated my disillusionment. The Jim who needed to get back to his dying mom shot straight. "May I speak freely?"

Julian leaned in. "Yes. Please."

"Your welcome kit is a total rip-off."

He blinked. Once, maybe twice. "Would you excuse me?"

Julian exited the room. I was sure I had offended him. Instead, he called his entire team into the room.

"Tell them what you told me," prompted Julian.

Surrounded by seven mega-successful executives, I felt like that kid taking out the trash in a burger drive-thru line all those years ago. Julian nodded at me as if to say; it's okay. I repeated what I had told Julian.

"Kits should be optional, or at least pack your kits with products, so distributors have samples to share with friends."

I then proceeded to double and triple-stack my opinions.

"Compensation plans should be based on customer acquisition, not recruiting. It's the only way to attract distributors who genuinely will be loyal to your company."

"There are too many hoops to jump through to get paid as a distributor. Pay a distributor well if they only get customers. Pay well if they decide to build a team. Don't force people to do one over the other."

"More than 80% of those who have access to the internet worldwide are on social media, and you're forcing everyone to do home parties and making everyone feel like there's no other way to build their business. That isn't true."

Two hours turned to eight. At one point, I argued with the CEO of one of the top nutritional supplement companies.

Julian ate it up. Biggest grin in the room. Getting on into the evening, he paced laps around the runway-length table and told his team they had failed the people—that this, what I was saying, was what they had been missing. Maybe not the coziest path to comradery, but I had earned the team's respect with a conversation on all way business must change to move forward.

This encounter with Julian and his team was one of the most transformative conversations I've had in my life. From that moment on, I refused to waver from being fearless and honest in all conversations.

A conversation works on social media

The second C to mastering my social media system is the conversation.

It's about having authentic and robust conversations about your personal and business life with your social media friends.

You want to have real conversations with those who might be interested in your business. It's not always easy. Maybe you have limited time, so making phone calls feels overwhelming. Maybe sending emails isn't giving you the results you seek. You now have a solution. By utilizing social media, your ability to have real conversations with others becomes second-nature. Using social media allows you to know when people have seen your conversations, make HD audio or video calls anywhere in the world, chat with people in a group setting, and much more.

Social media makes having authentic conversations with others, one on one or in a group setting, easy. Now is your time to engage in spirited and honest conversations that grow your business.

Yesterday's technology

In the early days, my team and I connected with new people online, through friends, via newspaper ads, business cards in fishbowls on restaurant counters, bulletin boards, yellow pages, and lead generation companies.

Our next point of contact was by phone. It wasn't always what we said on the phone but how we said it that made a difference. We often ruled over the kingdom of Foot-in-Mouth—wrong statistics, confused details, reinventing the business name. Surprisingly, it didn't matter. Our excitement was contagious. People wanted to learn more.

Most of the time we got a person's voicemail. We spoke from the heart. We told them our name and why we were reaching out then asked them to take action by getting back in touch with us. We called three times, maximum before we let them go.

Video calls didn't yet exist, so we met people face to face—coffee shops, restaurants, home parties, grand hotel meeting rooms.

Lastly, antiquated three-way calls were an excellent way to build deeper connections, but group calls presented challenges: coordinating schedules; some participants not having call waiting, which resulted in a busy signal; generally talking over each other and much repeating.

The platform may have changed, but the features have not.

Instead of your phone being a physical object, your phone is a button located on some social media sites. The image looks like a phone and acts as a phone. Tap it, and you're inside a phone call.

Voicemails on social media go wherever you take your phone. They are saved forever. Tap a play button and listen. You can even respond to the person by leaving a voicemail.

Face to face is still powerful, and you should meet people in person as often as possible. Via social media, however, you can have a heart-to-heart chat with anyone on the planet. Mind-blowing when you think about it, right? Also, the interaction happens faster because you didn't have first to align crazy scheduling conflicts and travel.

Text messaging also became a life-saver. When all else fails, you can quickly send text messages inside social media.

Today's technology

Today, three-way phone calls happen in group conversations on social media. Leave each other voicemails and texts to arrange a phone or video conference meeting. Everyone responds when they are available. This keeps the conversation going while schedules align.

Affording people the chance to hear your voice and see your facial expressions as you enthusiastically talk about your product or service is a big part of a successful business. Social media reaches this core better than any other form of technology. When done right, social media is the new standard of authentic conversation—perhaps even more potent than meeting people in person because time is flexible and relationships deepen at a pace that's organic to all parties.

Strengthening your conversation

Having real conversations with friends only works when you learn the psychology of social media. Understand why people think the way people think and watch your business soar using social media.

Prejudgment

I met a guy on social media named Ken. He suggested I use his business partner in India to set up a tech system I wanted to use to grow my business. I contacted Naveen, who quoted me a cost of $5,000 and a timeframe of four months. Two other estimates came in at $50,000 and $100,000, both with longer timeframes and additional hourly programming rates. Right about now, you're likely thinking about what I was thinking: five grand sounded too good to be true. I chose the middle of the road, a decision I came to regret. Wishing for a time machine kind of regret. Many delays and an hourly rate that bled my funds dry left me with broken infrastructure and enough software glitches to summon tears—ahem, masculine tears. I called Naveen. Even an eight-thousand-mile conversation couldn't mask the desperation in my tone. Naveen agreed to build the system for free. In return, he recouped his money by charging a monthly fee to access the system. He finished the work in three months, and it was perfection—no bugs, no glitches, no hassle. At this point, I would have married Naveen, but I settled for referring him to everyone I knew, without even a thought to compensation. Naveen is brilliant at tech but needed help with the business. We became good friends and business partners in another venture.

How many other social media friends of yours do the same? People are exquisitely complex, with diverse backgrounds and varied life experiences. Everyone has the potential to do business with you, even if they may not seem so at first glance. Never prejudge, no matter the temptation. It takes ten seconds to have a conversation with your friend on social media. Those ten seconds can mean the difference between new business or missed opportunity.

Real friends

Nolan is a pool shark. He challenged me to the best of three. Best of three ballooned to best of 21 because I am awful at billiards. Not only did the game extension afford me the chance to get to know a truly genuine person, but Nolan also received advice on ways to improve his business using social media. I was teaching him our social media system in a place he loved.

People who are in a comfortable environment are more open, more honest, more receptive to things that might be beyond their understanding. Think of social media as the pool hall of business. You meet people in their natural environment, surrounded by the comfort of their real friends. Take up residence in that zone first, as a friend, and your business will flourish.

Nolan and I live a few hours apart from each other. These days, we play virtual pool on social media, he's still a pool shark, and we do business together.

Life experiences

My friend, Jackie, is exceptional at entrepreneurship. I asked her to look at our social media system because it might help her. She said, "No thanks, Jim, but I appreciate you asking." Does she need our system? Definitely. Does she think she needs it? Definitely not. We have liked and commented on each other's social media posts and wished each other a happy birthday for the last few years. Jackie also trusts me. She knows I am passionate about social media and have the credibility to back up my words. Unfortunately, she has not yet had a life experience to make her think she needs our social media system.

A life experience is when someone has a background that opens her eyes to the importance of your product, service or business.

Fear of rejection

Mr. Secara taught senior year economics.

For an entire semester, I tried to pitch him my long-distance phone service. Each time I mustered the courage to darken his classroom door after school, I chickened out. Though Mr. Secara was kind and nurturing, I was a mess of rejection panic.

One day, I stood in the empty hallway for thirty minutes, listening to the sounds of him grading papers. I ran through a million scenarios in my head, most of them ending with Mr. Secara laughing or a fire alarm clearing the building. The bundle of marketing materials in my arms—brochures, presentation books, VHS tape— felt like an anchor that kept me from moving forward. I took one step in the room.

Mr. Secara glanced up. His expression illuminated, and he smiled. "Hey, Jim."

At eighteen, my small-talk skills left a little to be desired. I launched in like napalm, loud and messy. "Would you check this stuff out and tell me what you think?" I said then dumped my armload on his desk.

He said, "Sure."

I'll tell you that after he uttered that one word—sure—I bolted out of his classroom like someone had pulled the fire alarm — not my finest moment.

Fear of rejection is real, and I had an acute case of it in high school. The only reason I walked into that classroom was because I believed in my business.

Keep in mind that rejection isn't personal. When someone says no to your business, they're doing just that—saying no to business, not you.

Don't be aggressive

Maddie sends me a conversation on social media once a year with a new product for me to try. Each conversation is filled with excitement and goes like this: Hey Jim! It's Maddie. Listen, I found a product that is going to change your life. Can I tell you about it?

I usually say, "Hey Maddie. What happened to the last product or the product before that? You were just as excited about those products, and now you're no longer promoting them."

It's hard for me to have a conversation with Maddie because this has been going on for 15 years.

My other friend, Kathy, is the opposite of Maddie. Eighty percent of the time, Kathy talks to me as a friend. She reaches out to me from time to time on social media, asks how my family is doing and chats like a friend. Now and then, she reminds me of her business. I don't mind hearing about her business because I know she is my real friend. A day may come when I need a product like hers. I will order from her because she cares about me as a person.

Your business will always be there as long as the relationships with your friends are deep and meaningful.

Lighting up a conversation by being real

The catalyst of conversation is being the real you. Be the real you in your personal life. Speak from the heart and show confidence in your business life. You use your product or service daily. You know it works; therefore, it will work for others.

Personal life

Early in my life, my friends thought it would be best if I got a local job. I recall my closest high school friends taking me out for a drink at the bar a couple of years after high school graduation.

"Jim, you're an awesome guy, but you're shooting too big. We believe in you, but you're not going to make it. People like us don't get rich, and we don't change the world. Rich people change the world."

A few drinks later, the message shifted. "Stay in town with us. We can go out on the weekends. Have fun. Go to college down the road. By the time you get out of college, you can be bringing in $30,000 a year then maybe work your way up to $100,000 a year someday."

I'd had enough. Drinks. Skewed philosophies. Negativity.

"Listen up, guys. I love you. I have no idea how I am going to do it. I don't expect you to believe in me. However, I believe in myself. I know I can change the world. I know I can change my world. I know I'll fail a thousand times. I also know I'll succeed. I don't care about a job or what you guys say is job security. I also don't believe your rants about rich people. I deserve a great life, and so do all of you. Come with me. Let's do it together."

They looked at me as if I had recited the Declaration of Independence backward. We left that night in silence. I went my way, and they went their way. It's been more than 20 years since that night, and I haven't had a job since. I changed my world. More importantly, I changed the worlds of many others. Be the real you.

Business life

Be the real you in positive situations. Victoria sent me a friend request the other day and a message: Hey Jim! Love to stay in touch. It looks like we have similar hobbies.

I replied, Nice to meet you. I checked out your profile. It looks like we have more than 40 mutual friends, as well. I'd love to hear why you decided to reach out to me — looking forward to hearing from you soon.

Victoria wrote That was a fast reply! Social media suggested we should be friends. It looks like we are both entrepreneurs, so I thought why not? It looks like you've done well-growing business on social media. I've been an entrepreneur for the last five years. I would love to stay in touch!

This conversation went back and forth a few more times until I felt comfortable that she wanted to be a real friend. Friend request accepted and eventually, we did business together.

Be the real you in negative situations. I sent Cheryl a friend request on social media. She did not accept my friend request. Instead, she sent me a message on social media. The message read, Hi, Jim. I can't approve your friend request. I'm sorry. I'm happily married.

Huh? I was speechless. I replied, Hi, Cheryl. I'm glad you're happily married, as well. Did you happen to read my message that went along with my friend request? Please check it out. If you feel we could be friends, I'd love to hear back from you.

She responded I'm sorry, Jim. Please stop contacting me. I don't have time to check out your message. Again, I'm married. This doesn't seem right.

I responded, Be well, Cheryl.

Sometimes things make sense, and sometimes they don't. Time shaped my skills toward a great truth: how I made someone feel during our conversations was directly proportionate to success. I wasn't selling my products or services. I was fostering an emotional conversation—with me, with the product, with the life they hoped to enjoy by uniting with my business.

As Bruce Lee once said, "Honestly express yourself." You can't go wrong if you stay true to the real you.

Conversation tips

Here are some tips for growing your business from the second C - Conversation of my social media system.

Social media allows you to have genuine conversations. This is the primary reason it's possible to use social media as a way to have relationships with others that turn into business.

Enjoy these five proven ways to create stronger conversations with people who will become friends, customers and refer your business to others.

90-Day Test

What should you say to your existing friends when starting the conversation? It's based on what my team and I call the 90-Day Test. Simply stated, if it's been more than 90 days since you have spoken to your friend on social media, reestablish the relationship. If it's been less than 90 days, you probably have a relationship with that person, and it's okay to bring up your business. Let's break down the 90-Day Test.

More than 90 days

Think about friends outside of social media. If you haven't spoken to someone in three months, would you call your friend out of the blue and immediately start telling him about your business? Of course not. You would take the first 15 minutes to catch up on life. Catching up on life inside of social media is called reestablishing the relationship. It's going into social media, scrolling to the last conversation you had with your friend, checking the date-stamp (is it more than 90 days? – Yes) then sending a message like, Hey (friend)! It's been a while since we last chatted. How have you been? Go back and forth two or three times, talking about life, not your business. Your friend will learn about your business during the fourth C - Communication of my social media system.

Less than 90 days

You check the date-stamp, and your last conversation was a month ago. Both of you chatted about your children's upcoming basketball game. It sounds like you have a relationship. You might be ready to talk business.

You might say, Hey (friend)! I just wanted to reach out and let you know I've been using this skincare line on my face, and it works wonders. My skin feels great. It's also organic. I like it so much, and I decided to share it with others to get free products and earn some extra money. Would you have an interest in trying a sample?

What happened? You shared your testimonial of your product and a product fact. It doesn't matter the product or service. Everyone has testimony and facts to back up the quality of their product or service.

What if your business is what some people might consider a more complicated product or service to share with friends? Let's say you own a tax accounting business. Try, Hey (friend)! wanted to let you know I'm giving a 50% discount to all my social media friends who let me do their taxes next year. I've been able to save the average customer $6,700 on their taxes this year (your product fact). I'm very passionate about taxes (I know weird), but I love helping people. (Your product testimonial). Would you have an interest in learning more about how the 50% discount works?

Decision-making stages

Organize your friends into lists. As you reach out to your existing social media friends, each friend will be at a different step of deciding to do business with you. To better serve your friend, you should know your friend's decision-making stage. Here are the ones that work best for me.

Initially, your friends will go into one of two lists: Did not respond or rebuild relationship.

Rebuild relationship

You haven't spoken to these people in 90 days. Your goal is to catch up on life, not discuss business.

Did not respond list

All friends who did not go in the rebuild relationship list go into this list until your friends respond to you. Once they answer back, then you can put your friends into the prospects list.

Prospects

As your friends respond (ONLY those from the did not respond list), your friends will say yes or no to your offer. Your friends go into the prospects list regardless of their answer. If your friends took the time to respond to you, they are considered a prospect for your business, now or in the future. It means you have a relationship.

Samples/More information

As your friends go through my social media system, you will send your friends samples or more information, as well as add your friends to your social media community. If your friends are trying a sample or reviewing more information, add these friends into this list while keeping them in the prospect list. These are your hottest prospects—the ones most likely to do business with you.

Customers

When a friend orders your product or service, put your friend in the customer list. This allows you to stay in touch on a personal level with friends who use your product or service.

Social influencers

When a friend shares your product or service with others and decides to become a Social Influencer for your business, put this friend in your social influencers list. This allows you to stay in touch on a personal level with friends who refer your business to others.

Starting a conversation

How does a conversation move your relationships beyond personal and into income producing activities for your business? You never know when someone will be ready to do business with you, so starting a conversation is essential.

New friends

If starting a conversation with people in person is difficult for you, you're not alone. Social media makes this ice-breaker easy. The pressure to respond when someone is looking at you, in person, can be intimidating. On social media, you can take your time and think about what you want to say by reviewing a person's profile.

You're now starting conversations. When making decisions about how many times you should go back and forth with people or what should you say, put yourself in their shoes. How would you want them to interact with you?

Always try to reach out to new friends within 24-48 hours. When starting the conversation, an essential piece of advice is to start.

Here is a simple way you can start a conversation with new social media friends.

Reply with, Hey (new friend)! Thanks for accepting my friend request and responding to my message. I'm excited to build a friendship with you. Continue the conversation based on what she said in her message. Your objective is to have a real conversation.

Existing friends

Starting a conversation with current friends on social media is more natural than connecting with new friends for the first time. History is there. You have commented on each other's posts and interacted in other ways. However, there is a right way and wrong way.

Wrong way

I hadn't spoken to Adam for six months.
Adam is one of those cool guys. He has
traveled everywhere, knows everyone,
listens to eclectic music, and has a diverse
group of friends. I visited him once, and it
was a day to remember. In the morning, we
hung out with a group of guys from Asia,
talking about technology. In the afternoon,
we chilled with a group from Europe and
discussed meditation and yoga. By evening,
we jammed out with a bunch of his friends
at a back-in-the-woods type of
outdoor concert.

I thought Adam and I were fantastic
friends, so I reached out to him: Hey Adam!
How have you been? I found this shaving
cream that makes my face look and feels
fantastic. I've been using it for a few
months, and it's all-natural. Can I send you
a sample?

He replied, Nice to hear from you, too.
Ouch.

I had not spoken to Adam in six months.
When I reached out to him, I focused on
selling instead of reconnecting. In essence,
my misguided message conveyed to Adam
that he was not a friend, but a means to a
sale. To remedy my mistake, I responded
right away and changed the subject. A
month later, after much rebuilding the

relationship, Adam took a sample. He became a customer, as well. Adam could have blown me off, and I might have lost a friend. He gave me a second chance. You may not be so lucky.

Right way

I helped a skincare company grow a customer base using social media. I hadn't spoken to my friend, Linda, in more than three months. As much as I wanted to tell her about the company's pineapple lotion, I followed my social media system. Linda loved pineapple, and she loved lotions. Imagine how hard it was for me to hold back until we reestablished our relationship with each other.

I sent her a message that read, Hey Linda! It's been quite a while since we last spoke. How have you been? I've seen some of your travel posts. It looks like you are seeing the country.

She responded with, Hey Jim! Long time no hear. Life's been great, and I'm traveling with my hubby and enjoying life. We're in retirement, and I'm delighted you said hi. We are off to the next spot. Chat soon!

I wrote, Looking forward to seeing your travel pictures. I'm doing a little traveling myself. I am headed off to Colorado. See you around social media!

Two weeks later, she commented on one of my posts about the pineapple lotion and asked for a sample. She became a customer and eventually referred many people who also became customers and referred their friends as well.

Had I contacted her with business first, she may have thought of me as a salesman and not a friend.

Continuing the conversation

How does conversation continue beyond the initial contact and into a fruitful conversation that turns into business? It's a back and forth melody between you and your friend. It's about building a meaningful relationship, creating influence and figuring out if your friend has a life experience, and is ready to do business with you.

Follow up with your friends once a week for three weeks after your friends express interest in your business. Most importantly, keep the conversation going. You never know when someone will be ready to do business with you.

Imagine that after an entire year of talking to a friend they are finally ready to look at your business. Social media allows you a chance to review a full year's worth of conversation so you can enter into a meaningful discourse and deepen that relationship while the potential for new business is there.

Mockup of a conversation

Iain sends his friend, Sandra, a message to check out the social media system you are experiencing right now. He spoke to Sandra less than 90 days ago. She's had a life experience, so she is always looking for ways to grow her business. She likes Iain because they talk to each other as friends on social media, not just about business. She trusts Iain about growing business on social media because he uses the social media system with success.

Iain's message:

Hey Sandra! I wanted to let you know that I launched my social media system that teaches people how to grow a successful business on social media using the power of relationships. As you know, I have used this system for a long time, and it has allowed me to never run out of people to talk to for my businesses. Would you like to check it out?

Immediately, Iain puts her on the did not respond list as a starting point.

Sandra responds, Sure, Iain. I'd love to hear more.

Iain moves her to the prospect List.

Iain says, Excellent! May I add you to our social media group so that you can get all the information you need at your own pace?

Sandra says, Okay.

Iain moves her on the Sample/More info list.

Next time Iain reaches out to Sandra, Iain writes, Sandra! You're now in the social media group. Please check your social media notifications to find the group easily. Please check out our marketing video. It should give you everything you need to make a decision right away. Let me know if you have an interest.

A week goes by, and Iain does not hear from Sandra.

Iain sends Sandra a message. Hey Sandra! It's been a week since we last spoke. What do you think of the social media group?

Another week goes by with no response.

Iain sends her another message and says, Hey Sandra! Two weeks ago, you expressed interest in my social media system. Are you still interested?

A third week goes by. Still no response. Iain sends her the third message and says, Hey Sandra! I hope everything is okay. I haven't heard from you. Out of respect, I won't be sending you any more messages about my business. Just let me know if you change your mind. I am always here to help you. In the meantime, our friendship is the most important. See you around social media!

At any time during the conversation after Sandra is added to the social media group, Sandra may reply with interest. When Sandra replies, send Sandra a sample of your product, if that is an option.

If you send the sample too early, you will notice 1 out of every 20 people become a customer. If you send the sample after your friend expresses interest from the social media group, you will see that one out of every five people become a customer.

After you add Sandra to the social media group and she has questions, introduce her to a team member, if you have one or answer the questions yourself.

Create a social media group message between the three of you.

Hey Sandra! I'm excited you have an interest in our business. Your samples are on the way. Please ask my friend any questions you may have for the business. She's part of this group. Her name is Mary, and she's been using the product for about a year. She also builds this business full-time.

Mary, I'd like to introduce you to Sandra. Sandra has been in our customer social media group for the last week and is very interested. I sent her samples yesterday.

Mary will assist you in answering Sandra's questions, either via text, video or phone call or voicemail.

If Sandra says that she's not interested at any time during the conversation, Iain will not try to convince her to change her mind. Iain will say, May I ask why you are not interested? I will answer her concerns then thank Sandra for considering the business. The most important part of the conversation is keeping your relationship intact, not getting Sandra to become a customer or refer your business to others.

If your business has a social influencer program, it's vital that you ask Sandra to be a social influencer after she is ready to become a customer. Why? Your most active social influencers will be those who believe in the product or service. Think about it. If Sandra believes in your product, she'll easily share it with her social media friends.

A conversation is a series of coordinated steps that help your friends make an educated decision about doing business with you.

4 | Connection

Back in the 1990s, I was having a difficult time getting customers for my first business. At a time when deregulation of telecommunications was in its infancy, I continuously encountered loyalists who had been with the same phone company their entire lives. The idea of choice made them queasy.

Twenty minutes into most of my pitches, friends said, "Aw, Jimmy. I don't know. I've never heard of this company. I'm happy with what I am already using" Loyalist to the core.

However, John was different.

My friend's father, John, was a successful businessman. He sported three-piece suits from the big city, a fat gold watch, and shiny loafers with fancy stitching. I have no idea what he sold, but it wasn't door-to-door encyclopedias. As a young and inexperienced entrepreneur, I wanted a sliver of his success.

The day I pitched John long-distance phone service, I pulled my 1982 Nissan Maxima into his circular driveway and killed the loud, diesel engine. Next to the lion sculptures framing the front steps and the groomed rose bushes, I felt like a cheap flier stuck in the door seam—all but the black, faux-leather briefcase I had scraped together enough money to buy. The contents were of little consequence—pens, letters of authorization for my service, marketing brochures, a calculator because it seemed entrepreneurial. The case shined.

I dried my palms on my wrinkled chinos and rang the doorbell. Chimes bounded through the house beyond the glass door. More than once, I considered bolting. The man could afford a long-distance plan to the South Pole. What could he possibly want from an eighteen-year-old kid?

John answered the door in a polo shirt and golf pants. He smiled like he was on vacation, shook my hand the way he must have a million transactions in some high-rise in Philly—all let's-play-18-holes grip and a pump of reassurance.

The first ten minutes of my pitch, I could have floated the dining room table in sweat. My words poured out like a used car salesman.

"Take your time, son," John said. "You're doing great. I like what I'm hearing." I felt like I had surfaced after a near-drowning presentation. From then on, I took my time, stopped raking my hand through my then-hair, and chronicled examples of the remarkable savings my service brought past customers.

It turns out; John didn't want to spend his hard-earned money to call the South Pole. Saving forty bucks on long distance meant another round of golf. Also, golfers have friends. Lots of friends.

In six months, I had leveraged John's connections again and again and ended up with hundreds of customers to my service. Most called me in a month from signing up on the service to tell me thanks because they were seeing savings on their bill and then referred a few friends to my service. So there it was — the power of connections. John was the first one of my connections to hear my pitch and act—the man who could afford a long-distance plan to the South Pole.

A connection works on social media

The third C to mastering my social media system is a connection.

A connection is such a powerful word. The idea of connecting with others gets many people excited because, by nature, people are social. People want to be connected. As a kid, I remember going to the mall every weekend with my friends. Our only purpose was to meet as many people (okay, girls) as possible from the surrounding towns. The idea of connecting with people beyond our school was exhilarating. With few exceptions, my friends and I usually made three to five new friends on those weekends.

Quantity of connections

One common frustration businesses share is running out of people to talk to about their business. Maybe you already spoke to everyone you know. Worse yet, you don't know anyone who is looking for your product or service.

In the late 1990s, in a given week, my team and I got excited when we connected with 30 people using social media. It beat newspaper ads, fishbowls, and calling from the phonebook and my massive list of warm contacts. My biggest list was 120 people. Today, you can easily connect with ten to30 people per day using social media. Think about the last time you spoke to ten to 30 people about your business in a given day. If you're like most, you never have talked to this many people and now you can every day for the rest of your business career.

Connecting with ten new people a day is your new baseline. Are you feeling a little more ambitious? Connect with 20 new people a day. For those looking to build the biggest businesses in the shortest amount of time, focus on connecting with 30 new people a day. It's as easy as connecting with ten people in the morning, another ten in the afternoon, and your final ten in the evening.

Going above 30 people is not recommended because your intent is to build real relationships, not just for business. If you connect with too many people to fast, it will be difficult to develop real relationships with everyone.

Accessing an endless supply of potential customers and people who will refer your business to others, while building real relationships with real people, can happen using social media. Based on just one social media site's current user base, if you contacted 30 people a day for your business, it would take you more than 164,384 years to reach everyone the right way. When I say you'll never run out of people to talk to, I mean it.

Quality of connections

Let's look at it from the viewpoint of optimizing local to promote global growth for your business. Connection puts you in touch with everyone in the world who is on social media. Using connection at the local level, however, builds the most active businesses because you spend face to face time with people. Local relationships take your product or service around the world the fastest. Local is not just your hometown or current city—where you grew up or where you live now—but any place you have an opportunity to build relationships with people face to face. Increasingly, local relationships thrive on social media with features like video chat.

It's no surprise people feel more connected after spending time together face to face. People are social creatures. They want to be connected. Since a connection is so vital to our human experience, it makes sense to do business in environments where we have opportunities to meet others face to face.

The way you connect with people on social media is the same way you have always connected with people your entire life — just a new platform with an opportunity to connect with a lot more people.

Bolstering your connection

A connection may expose you to everyone, but it doesn't mean you become friends with everyone. Understanding three types of friends will help you connect with the right people. You don't want to find yourself with thousands of friends whom you don't really know and likely won't engage in a business way.

Close friends

The first tier of connections is close friends. You have the most in common with these people. If you live in your hometown, you may have grown up with these friends. Maybe you don't live in your hometown anymore. You moved away. Close friends in these new areas might be your coworkers, mutual friends of your spouse, or people with whom you share a common interest, like cooking. Maybe you went to the same high school or college and hung out together on the weekends. Maybe you virtually hang out in a social media group or met through a social media event around a shared interest. In all instances, these friends are part of your inner circle. They are the ones with whom you interact the most and close friends are more likely to do business with you over the other types of friends.

Six years ago, I lived in Scottsdale, Arizona. Alexanne and I became close friends. Not a weekend went by that we didn't hang out. We celebrated many holidays and special occasions together. Alexanne is the kind of person you'd want beside you if your business was on the line and a Fortune 500 CEO gave you an ultimatum: impress me or you're history. She's articulate and structured and poised when she needs to be and entirely down to earth and fun all the other times. I only know these details because she is considered a close friend. She's always open to what I have to share with her about business. Today, you'll find Alexanne and I talking about hot topics through social media even though we live more than 2,000 miles apart.

Acquaintances

The second tier of connections is acquaintances. Most of the time you're building your relationship through social media by liking and commenting on each other's posts. You like this person, but you don't have much in common. When something arises of common interest, you share it with this person. You continue your relationship on social media until the next common-interest occasion arises. She may never become a close friend; however, she will do business with you as soon as she has a life experience that relates to your business. You have a relationship because of the common interest. They respect your company because of your professionalism.

Rosemary and I have an age difference of 28 years. Our definition of fun probably differs, but we share a common interest. Rosemary and I both want to teach entrepreneurs how to be successful. Rosemary is a 40-year veteran in the small business community. Over the years, we spent time together and mostly kept in touch on social media. Whenever something arises that has to do with entrepreneurship, either Rosemary or I find ourselves reaching out to each other. Sometimes it's just to keep each other up to date with current trends and other times it is to share an opportunity. She is also a classy lady. Rosemary dresses to impress and uses the most eloquent words to explain herself—especially when talking about her passion for collecting antique cars. How do I know this? Because when we connect about entrepreneurship, we always take a moment to learn something about each other, so our relationship deepens beyond what brings us together.

People you don't yet know

The third tier of connections is comprised of people you don't know yet. You'll meet these people when you are out and about, through random chance, or social media connections. You can move someone from the third to second tier to the first tier in a short period with social media so long as you choose people to connect with that you'd want to be friends with outside of the business.

About five years ago, I traveled back to St. Louis, Missouri. While at the airport, I met an effervescent woman named Lisa with an infectious smile. Her large backpack suggested a Himalayan trek, but its familiar logo told me that we had the same event destination. We also realized we were both from Phoenix. We exchanged contact information and stayed in touch on social media. Over the last few years, we have built a cool relationship. Because of our geographical distance, I've only had a few face-to-face experiences with her. However, social media has allowed us to stay connected. Through social media, I learned that Lisa is an avid hiker—thus, the backpack—and volunteers her time to non-profit organizations that make people's lives better. Being supportive is second-nature to Lisa. She has learned a lot about me as well. We have developed an excellent relationship through social media.

Here is an example of how results might play out in your business:

- You meet ten new every day on social media. After a few months, you connect with 900 new people you don't yet know.

- 350 decides to stay connected with you because you have something in common. You now have new acquaintances.

- Six months later, 70 people decide to become your customer or refer friends to your business. Most of the time, customers are your acquaintances, and those who referred many friends to your business moved to close friends.

- Anna, one of your 70 customers, is ecstatic with the results of your product. She shares the product with Sarah, her close friend, on the other side of the country through social media because it is easy to do compared to calling Sarah. Anna is now referring your business to others, and

Sarah becomes a loyal customer because of the product benefits.

- Sarah tells Cindy, an acquaintance, about the product one day while chatting on social media. Cindy tries the product and also falls in love with the results. Cindy just so happens to live in another country.

This example happens over the course of 12 months with just one of your 70 customers. What if this scenario occurred with 20 of your 70 customers or all 70?

Whether you are talking to your close friends and acquaintances or meeting someone for the first time, creating connections through social media makes it easy to meet others. That ease makes it effortless to share your business with friends.

Amplifying connection with numbers

The catalyst of connection is numbers. I went to college for Entrepreneurship and Finance, where I learned the age-old wisdom that to be successful in any business, you need to know your numbers. Production costs, expenses incurred to sell the product, price points, and so much more comprise these all-important figures. Without understanding numbers, how does a business know if it is performing well or failing? Connecting with others using social media is no different.

Rule of 20

After decades of personal success, helping millions of people start their own business, my friend and mentor, Mark Yarnell, concluded that in order to build a successful business using word of mouth, you need to understand for every 20 people exposed to a business the right way, one would be excited enough to share the business with friends.

I put Mark's numbers to the test, and the numbers worked. Over the course of two years, using my social media system and his mentorship, I connected with 12,000 people. These numbers equated to 600 people who helped me promote my business.

Rule of five

Today, the numbers are even better. Instead of 20 connections needed to gain that one coveted person to refer your business to others, the desired person can be obtained using social media in only five connections.

As a small business owner, you're busy. Nearly every business task falls on your shoulders. Do you have twenty minutes in your day to connect with ten new people on social media? Sure. Think long term. In 30 days, you will connect with 300 people. In six months, it grows to 1,800 people. Over a year, you will connect with 3,600 new people. Based on our proven one out of five numbers, this equates to 60 new customers monthly and 720 customers after one year. What other marketing strategies can help you connect to this many people, build trusted relationships, and retain them as customers, all without spending money?

Understanding the numbers allows you to stay consistent at growing your business using social media.

New connections lead to new business, so consistently making new connections is key to your success. Not understanding the numbers aspect of making new connections using social networking will stifle growth.

So how did I come to the reality that the catalyst of connection was numbers?

Simple. Human behavior is unpredictable. The numbers are predictable. Social media has billions of people, making it the perfect playground for never running out of people to talk to for your business.

Connection Tips

Here are some tips for growing your business from the third C - Connection of my social media system.

Social media allows you to connect with people with whom you would instinctively connect in the real world. This is the primary reason it's possible to build meaningful relationships as strong as people make when meeting face to face.

Enjoy these eight proven ways to unlock new connections with the right people to create healthy relationships and new business.

Early school days

You might be thinking that you graduated too long ago or that you didn't have many high school friends. Maybe you didn't graduate at all. These common concerns disappear quickly for you as you start to reconnect and realize some people have changed and some have not. Others, you'll be surprised to learn, are just like you.

The common connection of going to the same high school makes the trusted relationship happen faster than meeting a stranger.

It's always wonderful to watch people's expressions light up because they reconnect through social media with those forgotten over the years. Life may have pulled them in different directions from their friends, but social media can be the great unifier.

A couple of years ago, I reconnected with Raymond on social media. The most persistent memory I have of Raymond is traveling beside him on a school bus to a field trip in fourth grade. We played a travel game of magnetic checkers and hung out together all day. Raymond and I had known each other since kindergarten, but our interests diverged about halfway through our school career. He was gifted with taking cars apart and putting them back together, and I gravitated more toward the baggy-pants, hip-hop crowd. I hadn't had a connection with him since eighth grade.

After a few months of staying in touch on social media, Raymond sent me a message: Hey Jim, I noticed you are doing well as an entrepreneur, and it looks like you're doing something with building a business on social media. At work, I had some friends introduce me to a business opportunity. I'm not sure if these opportunities are any good. My wife and I would love to make some extra money. Can you help?

Think about the significance of this message. Raymond and I hadn't spoken in 22 years. We had engaged in each other's posts weekly for a few months. He has friends at work, likely going years back, yet he asks me for a referral. Why? It's about trusted relationships. Time passed, but the trust never disappeared.

Raymond and his wife sampled a few products I referred and chose the one that gave his family the best results. His family now builds a fun, part-time business.

College

Not long ago, I reconnected with a college friend, Ryan. He was one heck of a chef, a ladies man, and never seemed to have a dull day. Ryan was one of those cool guys on campus. As with most college friends, careers got in the way, and we drifted apart. Since reconnecting on social media, we've stayed in touch. After six months of nurturing the relationship on social media, Ryan sent me a message.

What's up? I know I teased you about all those business deals you had going in college but look at you now. From what I see you posting on social media, you're killing it. I always knew you'd do something with all those crazy entrepreneurial ideas. I'm looking to do something new. Can you help me or put me in touch with someone?

As in early school days, trusted relationships take root in college. Ryan and I connected the right way on social media, which eventually led to me helping him. I referred him to the right people, and now he is following his passion.

Once, I challenged myself to see how far back in time I could go and still create a connection. I found a guy who graduated from my college, so I sent him a message: Hey Charles! It looks like we both went to Johnson and Wales University. The only difference is you graduated in 1975, and I went to school from 1999-2002. I hope to connect.

Charles responded with intrigue. We had connected about how much the campus had changed and what new majors were available. I am still friends with Charles today.

Attending the same college builds trusted relationships. Something worth pursuing.

Hometown

Hometown connections can expose you to hundreds of thousands of people, depending on where you live. These people all have the same roots as you. The deeper the connection, the more profound the relationship. The deepest relationships do business together in the most significant ways.

My hometown has a population of 19,000. When you add in the nearby towns, the population rises to 60,000. An hour away from my hometown is a city with a population of 250,000. In just these three areas, if I connected with 30 people a day, seven days a week, it would take me more than 30 years to contact everyone!

My friend Martha grew up in a hometown of 700 people. She wanted to connect with her current town because the population was 5,000. I said, "Give it a try. Look at it this way–there are only 700 people. You will connect with these people in no time, and you can use it as experience before you start connecting with everyone in your current town of 5,000."

Within a few weeks, Martha's feedback was fantastic. She told me story after story of how she connected to hometown people: how she forgot about someone, how someone else moved to a bigger town but was able to find another person because of a mutual friend from that town of 700. Not only did she reconnect with many friends, but her business also grew to nearby cities that had populations in the hundreds of thousands. Her confidence grew exponentially. All of this happened from a hometown of only 700 people.

Current city

It's possible to connect with a significant amount of people in your current city, depending on the city's population. This group can yield successful connections because you can combine the power of social media with the ability to meet people in person.

Do you want to connect with others who live close? Sure, you do! You crave a connection, just like everyone else. Having the opportunity to meet someone face to face provides the strongest sense of connection.

I met Erin at a coffee shop because a friend referred her to me. My friend told me that Erin was someone I needed to know in town because she was one of the most networked women in Scottsdale, Arizona. Within a month, Erin had sent me more than a dozen referrals. Ten of those referrals became customers.

We both lived in Scottsdale, and I wanted to do business locally. I had the opportunity to spend an hour with Erin, getting to know her and building trust and then staying in touch with her on social media. Had this happened today, I might have jumped on a video chat and reviewed all her social media profiles before meeting her for coffee to make sure we had a connection.

Over this past year, I met with several people in my current city who used our social media system. I notice these people interacted with me more on social media since meeting me in person. I do the same. Face-to-face, physical time invites deeper connections. Current city allows that to happen.

Interests

Common interests allow you to connect with people who might already have an interest in your type of business. Making connections with those who share common interests can result in an endless supply of friendships and new business.

This way of finding people connects you with others who already buy products or services similar to yours. If someone is already buying, they might consider buying from you—assuming your offer is comparable in quality and price—because you are trying to establish a relationship.

I once had a dental care business. I never thought I could get excited over toothpaste. However, this toothpaste felt great compared to what I was using at the time. I had that fresh, clean feeling after brushing. The mouthwash gave a tingling feeling when I gargled. Wonderful products. I stayed connected with Don through social media because we were both entrepreneurs with similar interests. I thought he would be an excellent candidate to expand my business into a new area, not just because he was a breathing mammal who brushed his teeth, but because we always talked about working together. I shared the products, and he liked them. I asked Don if he would be interested in expanding these products throughout his area. He jumped on the opportunity. In four months, Don produced $100,000 in product sales. That's a lot of toothpaste and mouthwash.

Connecting with people who already buy similar products can evolve into new business. If someone is already buying the same product or service and you are convinced your product is better quality and price, then this person should be your customer.

Mutual friends

You may have heard the phrase "six degrees of separation." It's the idea that it takes six or fewer connections (a friend of a friend) to connect with anyone in the world.

According to research done on social media in 2016, each person in the world (social media users only) is connected to every other person by an average of three and a half other people. Social media has redefined the idea of mutual friends by making the world a smaller place. Mutual friends can connect you to everyone on social media.

I am friends with Doug and Chris. Doug is a successful business owner doing over $1 billion in sales throughout his business career. He loves people and is always helping and serving others. Chris owns a magazine and founding member of a trade association. The trade association conducts an annual, three-day event where members come together for training and coaching. I wanted to be on the social media panel to help those in his profession since I had just published my first book and hit #1 bestseller status on Amazon.

I connected with Doug and informed him of the Amazon news. He wrote an endorsement for my book. Doug planned to speak at the trade association annual, three-day event. I asked if he would be kind enough to recommend to Chris that I sit on the event's social media panel.

At the same time, I connected with our mutual friend, Daren. He is an intelligent businessman who challenges the status quo with his forward-thinking principles. I asked him to pass along the same recommendation to Chris since Daren was already scheduled to speak on the social media panel. Daren also wrote a book review of my first book.

Next, I connected with Amber. People adore her for her candid social media videos in which she chronicles the transformation of her business from humble beginnings in a trailer to a seven-figure annual income. She was scheduled to appear on the social media panel, so I asked her to recommend me to Chris. Amber wrote me a book endorsement, as well.

I then connected with Evan. He magnetizes people to him with his German accent and a set of unbelievable singing pipes he only uses for fun. Evan knows and talks to everyone. A total social bee. Because he was also featured on the event's social media panel, I requested he recommends me to Chris.

Within one week, four out of the five people already approved to speak on the social media panel connected with Chris and told him I needed to appear on the panel with them. Final result? I was on the panel. Having mutual friends turns into business. Chris knew me enough to know I was a good guy but not enough for me to call him directly and ask to be on the panel.

All of these people who helped me speak on the social media panel I met through social media and stayed in touch using my social media system.

Groups

People love to connect with others who share commonalities. Think about your closest friends. What do you have in common? You probably like similar food, clothes, or places to go to.

Social media groups allow others to connect with people who have similar commonalities. You can connect with people just like you, 24 hours a day, seven days a week, from your laptop or phone. The days of being friends with people simply because you live close are over. You can now connect with people that you love being around because you have something in common.

A friend of mine once connected me to her social media group where people supported each other on all things business-related. A few months later, I saw a post from a member of this group: Can someone give me advice about how to use social media to grow my business?

By the time I read the post, it had more than thirty comments. Some answers were well-intentioned but misguided, and others were flat-out wrong. I jumped in and wrote a few sentences. Within days, I had a few people from the group who had read my comment reach out to me privately to tell me how much my perspective resonated with them — genuine, ambitious business owners who had a fire in their hearts to elevate their achievements. As a result of that one comment, I made four new friends who were passionate about business.

Using groups, I've been able to find those interested in two of my favorite passions, martial arts, and entrepreneurship.

Events

Social media events are a fantastic resource to build pre-relationships, connect with people face to face, and continue relationships online. Find out what's going on in your local area and who are attending the events. Reach out and establish a friendship before the event starts. Then you can attend the event already knowing people.

I used to be a business event junkie. I love connecting with like-minded people, and these semi-local events fueled my appetite for networking. I rarely made more than a few key connects. Almost always, I came home absent a bunch of business cards with no real follow up from myself or the people I met. I needed a better strategy.

A winning strategy turned out to be a small investment of time on the front end of each event by using the event feature found on social media sites. Not only did I gather advanced information about events that I wanted to attend, but events also expanded my awareness of other meet-ups. Also, I browsed through the list of those who planned to participate in an event, searching for those with whom I believed I had a great deal in common and could build a relationship first, business connection second. For future attendees who fit that criteria, I reached out to them privately. Those who replied became an event priority for me.

Events were now selective and strategic. I no longer wasted time. Now, in a room of one hundred people, ten were already primed to meet in person. The quality of our interaction elevated, as well. Because I had visited these people's social media profiles to become familiar with their likes and interests and had already established a connection via social media, our in-person time strengthened our connection exponentially. After the event, we continued to grow our relationship. Almost always, in time, these relationships evolved into new customers for my business.

5 | Communication

Donovan King is the crown prince of business leap-frogging. No pond is as great as the one Donovan occupies at any given time. When business gets murky, he jumps fast and far and tries to convince those around him to do the same.

More than a decade ago, Donovan and I shared business lines. We kept in touch through social media, but Donovan was slippery. When he surfaced, it felt like an ambush, one of those biblical plagues where my social media feeds were all-consumed by his latest—and always best—venture. Instead of riiiiiibittt-riiiiibittt, Donovan's communication sounded like meee, meee, meee. I tired of the incessant self-noise and quieted my interaction with Donovan's posts, though I remained close enough to track his leap-frogging. Donovan slipped into other ponds, and we lost touch.

Several years ago, I attended an awards ceremony with a friend, Elizabeth. I was so proud to be in the audience, to play a supportive role, to watch her shine as she walked across the convention stage to collect her award for being a high producer. At the reception after the ceremony, Donovan leaped near me.

"Oh my God, Jim. It's been years." Donovan's eyes were wild with lost time. "I didn't know you were part of this business."

"I'm not. I'm here to support Elizabeth."

We made formal introductions for the benefit of our companions. Donovan launched into the self-noise. He spoke about how successful he had been with Elizabeth's company. He relayed all the things and places and highlights that constituted his absence in my life. I began to hear it all again. Meee, meee, meee. He tried to convince me to jump ponds with a nearly unprecedented offer: several million dollars of sales volume to be given to me for future commission payouts. It guaranteed a sizable six-figure a year income with little effort from me.

I politely declined. "This is Elizabeth's day to shine. I want to focus on her success today."

Because Donovan viewed life and relationships through a very narrow lens that always included him, he didn't listen. He flattered and pushed until I knew I had to pull him aside. I put my arm around his shoulder, and we excused ourselves to the courtyard.

"Donovan, you should know me well enough to know I'm not about the money. I want to change the world. I want to help people find their success. Relationships are the most important commodity to me."

"Think about all the new relationships you'll have if you join me," said Donovan.

Mee, mee, mee.

He still didn't get it. I tried to stay in a mental place of gratitude for all we had experienced together. However, I was drowning in Donovan. I wanted to get back inside, to get caught up in the moment of Elizabeth's achievements.

"You should have stayed in communication with me, Donovan and asked how I was doing from time to time. That's why Elizabeth is on another team in the company. Relationships above all, man."

Donovan is a good guy. I am who I am today because of the relationships I have amassed in business and life—Donovan included. He means well. However, Donovan is a cautionary tale for those who filter their understanding of the world through a narrow, self-absorbed lens. Perhaps he believes the best way to relate to someone is to convey that he, too, has had a similar life experience. However, all the time Donovan is talking about things he already knows, he's not listening for new ideas, new perspectives.

A communication works on social media

The fourth C to mastering my social media system is communication.

Effective business communication is about how to stay in touch the right way so that you can build enduring relationships. Growth of relationships means you will always have an endless list of people who may look to your business.

The past

Let's track back to what worked for me early in my social media journey. Maybe you have done the same—Email, meeting in person, and phone calls. Those same methods are possible and more successful now thanks to today's social media parameters.

In my early business days, someone told me that most people have a reasonably significant life experience every six months. A shift in employment, living situation, income, personal relationships, and health concerns are just some transitional life events that might open up potential customers and people who want to refer your business to others. As such, contacting every six months from the last time you spoke with people is optimum to capture this transitional window. Reaching out to people every six months is one of the best ways to capture this window of opportunity. Eventually, they will do business with you.

At that time, follow up with social media was limited because the technology was still in its infancy. People came and went. Not many parked in the same spot on the internet, so follow up with people I met through social media was a little like nailing Jell-O to the wall. I met a lot of new people, but I wasn't able to stay in touch. Also, chatting and forums dominated social media. Sifting through communication threads became tedious. My solution was to forge a relationship with new people then ask them for their email address. I collected a nice batch of emails. About 20% of the people who gave me their emails also gave me phone numbers. These steps worked well.

Email follow up, however, felt like a one-way street. People knew nothing about me but what I had written in text—black and white, no emojis, no photos—and there was no guarantee they would reply. My relationship-building toolbox needed more. I emailed out a monthly update to everyone on my list in the hopes that when I approached the six-month time, people would give me their phone number so that we could have real communication.

I became addicted to collecting email addresses from people I met in person and through social media. At one point, I had tens of thousands of email addresses I gathered, not purchased through email lead generation companies. My contacts received an email from me once a month. Every six months from the time I last spoke with them, like clockwork, many would ask me to call them to have communication about all the emails that they have been receiving in the months prior.

Meeting with people in person was my least favorite follow up strategy because it was time-consuming and slow.

Consider the following.

I call Oscar on Monday. Oscar is busy being grouchy, so he doesn't return my call until Tuesday. I ask Oscar when he's available, but Oscar has a busy week. We agree to meet the following Monday. By the time our meeting comes around, an entire week has passed. As such, I only did this follow-up meeting with those who were the most important to me in terms of becoming a customer or refer my business to friends, though Oscar might have benefitted from a little social interaction especially if I was selling happiness.

Phone calls were my favorite. They combined the power of social media, emails, and meeting someone in person with a more instant and ideal timeline. I consistently made between 100 and 200 phone calls every weekday to talk to 30 new people per day. Then I made another 100-200 phone calls to follow up with 30 people I had spoken with during the six months prior. When I added a phone dialer, my productivity rocketed. I wore a headset and carried a remote phone in my pocket. Sexy, I know. The dialer made calls and left voice mails for me using my pre-recorded voice. People never picked up their phone, but the dialer connected me live if someone answered. With this system, I breezed through my daily list in three to four hours instead of six to eight. The only drawback to phone calls over in-person meetings was my inability to read facial expressions and body language, so I trained myself to listen for vocal inflections and word cues.

I started my phone communication as follows:

"Hey (name)! This is Jim Lupkin. I spoke to you six months ago about trying my product and maybe referring it to others to earn some extra money for yourself. Do you remember me?"

Most of the time, the person said, "Of course. How are you?"

I'd say, "I'm doing well. I want to hear about what's going on in your life."

Often, people shared a problem or struggle. I listened to their life experience to determine if my business could help them find a way through a difficult time. When—and only when—we had rekindled our relationship, I added, "I'm so glad we had this opportunity to catch up. I'd love to let you know what I've been up to since the last time we spoke. Is that okay?"

Person: "Sure."

I'd say, "Great! Well, since the last time we spoke, my business has (give an update on what you accomplished since the last time you spoke).

The present

With social media, the platform has changed; but the principles remain the same.

Then: You collected email addresses and potential phone numbers.

Now: You collect social media friends. These friends have a lot more on their profiles than emails and phone numbers.

Then: You sent a boring, black-and-white email once a month, informing all of your prospects what happened in your business the previous 30 days.

Now: You post colorful and emotion-driven pictures and videos on social media daily, which gives your friends more reasons to do business with you, sooner rather than later. These posts and videos share your personal life, which builds real relationships that convert to new business faster.

Then: Every six months, since the last time you spoke to someone, a good amount of contacts would ask you, via email, to call them or meet with them in person because they had a life experience. They had seen your emails for the previous five months. Most days, you would make 100-200 phone calls to connect to 30 people with whom you spoke precisely six months ago by phone. If they were your most valuable prospects, you set up a time to meet with them face to face. If not, your entire communication was limited to the phone.

Now: People may still ask you to call. However, many people today prefer you communicate with them directly inside social media and are willing to communicate back in social media without a phone call. Instead of waiting every six months to have communication about your business, you can talk about your business weekly, professionally, using social media. As people like and comment on your business posts, it allows you to follow up with people a lot sooner than six months.

Additionally, you can still communicate to people with whom you haven't spoken in six months, except now you can leave them voice mails inside of social media, the equivalent to leaving a voicemail on the phone. Leaving voice mails inside social media is faster, and people are more likely to respond to the voice mail than to phone you back.

Lastly, you can still meet your most important prospects face to face, either in-person or via a video chat on social media.

Every successful business person knows that the fortune is in the follow-up. One day, your contact will have a life experience that opens his eyes to your product or service. Staying in touch in the interim via social media is the key to success. When done correctly, follow up is effortless, consistent, and professional. Potential business rarely falls through the cracks.

Intensifying your communication

Social media makes maintaining real communication with others easy, and it's a more effective tool than emails, calling lists, drum circles, and anything and everything that exists today, both online and off-line.

I had finished the month of December with great outreach numbers. Despite connecting with 600 new people for my business, only 30 moved forward to do business with me. Five hundred and seventy people decided not to move forward because they did not yet have a real relationship with me, trust my knowledge of what I was doing, or have a life experience deep enough to make them realize my business could help them.

Every month from January to June, like clockwork, I communicated with these 570 people. The goal was to build a relationship, so they trusted my judgment and would be ready to enter into business with me when they had a life experience related to my business.

By June, I had moved to Florida. Most days, I sat poolside with my phone and worked on my computer. Sometimes I floated on an inflatable with a glass of iced tea making calls. At the time, I thought of this practice as brave. Brave isn't the word I'd use now.

My business ran a June promotion. I wanted to win even more than I wanted to look Hollywood, floating in that pool. At 9 am, I pulled out my list of 570 contacts with whom I had faithfully communicated every month since the previous December. I reached out to all 570 in 24 hours. I won the promotion. I helped 18 people, who had previously told me no, become a distributor in my network marketing business with me that day, and I helped even more become customers. I had put in the time between January and June to stay in touch and build relationships. As a result, we all won.

Here's what I learned.

Time matters

It's essential to stay in touch with people because real relationships take time. People must like you if they're going to do business with you. Some people will genuinely like you within minutes. For most people, that relationship takes longer to build.

Past experiences matter

How much and how quickly someone trusts you are mostly based on parameters beyond your control. Every interaction in that person's past has conditioned them to hold to beliefs about trust, both positive and negative. Some people grow up in a world where they were protected and supported; therefore, the rate at which they build relationships is faster than someone who grew up in an environment where their trust was often betrayed. Additionally, their history of dealing with business people in the sales arena might be clouded by those who have not been good stewards of their trust in the past. Understand that you may be inheriting broken trust when building a relationship.

Longevity matters

In my experience, the fastest way to build trust is to stay with your business and not start another one. Longevity in business suggests a continuation in relationships. Stay in touch with your friends. Offer updates of all the progress that you're making in your business. I have been doing social media for more than a quarter of a century. I never changed course. Trust is high when I talk about this subject.

Simplicity matters

First, speak at an eighth-grade level on social media—most of the time. People like and comment more when you don't whip out the silver-dollar words. I don't want you to dumb down your posts. Be yourself. Think of social media as the level of discourse you have when a bunch of your friends takes you to lunch.

Likes matter

Most people like posts because they don't have anything meaningful to add to a conversation. Other people might be shy, busy, or don't want to share. Likes mean that people are genuinely starting to like you. Likes are good.

Comments matter

People comment on posts because they have something meaningful to say about the content and are willing to spend the time to share their thoughts. Comments are a symbol of trust, either from a personal or a business perspective, or both.

Controversial topics matter

Please don't attack people for their beliefs on subjects like religion and politics. Do you want your voice to be heard or do you want to build your business? In these polarizing times, the two realities are often mutually exclusive. Focus instead on valuing the relationships and celebrating the communication between friends. The same applies when engaging on others' controversial posts. Stay neutral, and you'll maintain the trust you've worked so hard to build.

Emotions matter

Focus on feelings most of the time and facts some of the time. The emotional drive in humans often overpowers common sense. Sprinkle your interaction with occasional facts, and this heart-first tactic will concrete anyone's decision to do business with you. Connect with people, heart first.

Positivity matters

Being positive always trumps negativity. If you are a positive person who focuses only on going up, not down, you'll inspire many people to become good friends. Even in the most negative of situations, positivity can be found.

Life experiences matter

You don't have to be a salesperson to succeed. What keeps someone committed to your business is when this person understands the real value your product or service offers and wants it in their life. Selling to someone without this person having had a life experience relating to your product or service is a hamster wheel. Once you sell, you will always need to sell to that person, so they continue to do business with you. You have conditioned these people to believe you will do most of the heavy lifting in the relationship. However, if you nurture the relationship until someone has a life experience, your business interaction achieves a balance between what you offer and what life is telling your friend he or she needs.

Boosting communication with trusted relationships

The catalyst of communication is relationships. Think about your most loyal customers and those who refer your business to others. Likely, these people have a trusted relationship with you. Building trusted relationships while using social media is a foundational piece to your business success.

Many years ago, I wanted to get in front of as many people as possible and share my business. The idea of building trusted relationships with others was foreign. I had a difficult time comprehending why others would want to be so close to me before making a purchasing decision. I lost many promising people because I never cared to build trusted relationships.

Recognize the boundaries

Mark and I were best friends. He was the first person I asked to join me in my early business ventures. We contacted his family and friends to pitch our service. I was aggressive with my style, pushing and scrapping for every morsel of business interest I could generate. Mark's friends were my means to an end. One night, over his grandmother's delicious old-world Italian feast, a dinner I barely tasted because I was so focused on closing deals with the family gathered at the table, Mark put his fork down and said, "I'm done."

He wasn't talking about the fifteen-layer lasagna.

Mark decided not to move forward in business with me because he valued his relationships more than business. I was too assertive with his family. Looking back on those times, I believe that if I had focused on relationships, Mark could have been successful with me. He cared about people. Since those days, Mark has gone on to build beautiful relationships, both professionally and personally. He's always done right by people. As a result of the relationship-building skills he demonstrated more than two decades ago, Mark now holds a leadership position with a major company.

The stronger a relationship, the more likely one party will purchase goods or services from the other. Consumers are looking for products and businesses that they can trust and that have earned their loyalty. Your ability to build and maintain a healthy relationship with your customer will influence their buying decisions, customer loyalty, customer satisfaction, and customer retention.

Mutual respect and support are essential. Both people in a relationship need to have a sense of fulfillment. It's as easy as taking a genuine interest in others. Take the focus away from you. In your lifetime, you may have heard the phrase, "Listen more than you talk." It's the motto of every successful person within any industry.

Respect the boundaries

Another promising business partner I lost early in my first entrepreneurial venture was David. For him, the business was about personal development. He was shy and awkward around strangers. At one event, he even knelt to the ground and pitched our service to a girl no older than ten because he was too shy to pitch to adults. Though we were peers, equal members on the same team, the higher-ups in the company often invited me to speak on stage at events. Important people began to notice me for things beyond the thrift store clothes and government assistance of my past. My ego swelled.

While traveling with David and two other team members to an event in Baltimore, I took a phone call in the airport shuttle that ran long. The van stopped in front of our hotel. I glanced at David and said, "Hey! Grab my bags and bring them to my room." I finished my call poolside.

After, in the hallway outside our rooms, David's shyness was no longer present. He paced the geometric patterns in the carpet. His voice overpowered the drone of housekeeping's vacuum a few doors down.

"I'm here because I believe in you, but you can't treat me like this."

I glanced at the suitcase he'd placed outside my door. At that moment, getting sucked up in the vacuum rollers would have been preferable to facing the inconsiderate person I had become. My behavior was unacceptable. Worse, I had ordered him around in front of a group of people. I went to Baltimore believing David could learn a few things from me, but David taught me a more important lesson. Although I apologized many times, David and I grew apart because he no longer felt equal in our business relationship.

Ultimately, I learned

Shortly after my experiences with Mark and David, I started reading personal development books. One of the first books I read was How to Win Friends and Influence People. The author, Dale Carnegie, said, "You can make more friends in two months by becoming interested in other people than you can in two years by trying to get other people interested in you."

Personal development books and mentors who understood this space opened my eyes to the meaning of building trusted relationships. I've taken these experiences and applied them to my social media system.

It has allowed me to build deeper relationships than I ever thought were possible. Communicating with people, I would naturally seek out as friends, leading with the intent of making a meaningful relationship, creating purposeful messages and showing gratitude towards my newfound friendships are just a few ways of building real relationships using social media.

Your business will succeed faster if you focus on building trusted relationships. These relationships happen quickly when you take a genuine interest in others. Make the other person the focus of your energy. Listen more and talk less. When you get an opportunity to share your experiences, do so openly and excitingly so that your friends can paint a picture of the type of person you represent. If others see you for the authentic and honest friend you are, they will quickly pay for your product or service and refer your business to others.

Communication tips

Here are some tips for growing your business from the fourth C - Communication of my social media system.

Social media allows you to communicate with people for many years to come. This is the primary reason it's possible to follow up with people on social media.

Enjoy these seven proven ways to create stronger communication with people who will eventually do business with you.

80/20 rule

Posting on social media sites is about giving your friends a sneak peek into your personal and business life using an 80/20 principle because your friends care more about you than your business. The 80/20 rule has worked successfully for me for many years. Stated, 80% of your posts should be about your personal life and 20% of your posts per week should be about your business.

Remember, people do business with you when they like you, see you as someone of influence with your type of business, and have a life experience. People can only like you if they see you as a friend and have a relationship with you. Friends can only be nurtured on a personal level. Friendships take time to develop, which is why dedicating the majority of your time to grow these relationships makes good business sense. Since most people only have a life experience, on average, every six months, it makes sense only to spend 20% of your posts on business. Doing more business posts is not going to speed up someone's life experience. However, doing more business posts may push your friends away. They will think you're all about business and will be turned off by the prospect of building a relationship with you.

Personal posts

Personal posts should comprise 80% of your posts. Share what holds meaning for you—deaths, births, events that make you smile, something your child did that frazzled you, a small gesture your spouse does to light up your day. Share random thoughts you have as you're walking down the road and notice the wind against your cheeks. Share weddings and parties and joy. It's not about whether or not you have an exciting or dull life. We all have exciting experiences when we value what's right in front of us. Let your friends know what is right in front of you. That is how relationships take root and grow.

Sharing all aspects of your life is essential. It's common for a mother to post a lot about her children. It's common for a single guy to post about all the parties he attends. It's common for a businessperson to only post about business-related experiences. Isn't there more to you? Are you one dimensional? If you only show one side of you, then that is the only thing you will be known for. The best relationships are built when you show all aspects of your life to others. If you're a mother with children, you may also like to write poems in your spare time. Share those with your friends on social media. If you're a single guy, you also might be into cars. Show off your favorite cars to your friends on social media. You might think you're all business, but you also might like to run. Take pictures along the path of your favorite route.

How do you write a great personal post? Lead with your emotions, open your heart, be honest, genuine and transparent. Remember those moments when you let down your guard. Think of a time you cried and let it all out, or a moment you laughed so hard you struggled to draw breath. Remember those moments. Each time you write a post, strive for these beautiful emotions.

Here are examples of my posts over one week:

- Love being silly with her. (image: Marianne standing beneath a giant iron horse)

- Family first. Miss you nana. My grandmother passed in 2013. Always think about her. She's sitting in this picture. (image: my grandmother and family at a family picnic 20 years ago)

- I'm still wondering why I had a boxing session with this cactus on my hike. Sometimes, I do the weirdest things. (image: I am boxing a cactus)

- Mason puts this puzzle together effortlessly, all by himself. It amazes me what he can do for just turning three years old. (image: Mason on the floor putting together a puzzle)

- If you could pull anything out of this blue cup, what would it be? (image: I am sitting at a coffee shop holding a blue cup)

Business posts

Business posts should comprise 20% of your posts. Business posts can focus on facts, emotions, or a combination of both. The most effective business post you can write is a post about what has happened in your life involving the business during the previous week. These business testimonials originate from the heart and tap into your emotions, which, in turn, tap into your friends' feelings. Here, I'll share an example of each of the four types of business posts: Personal, Weekly, Educational, and Ask Your Friends. Please do not use these examples word for word. Insert your words, your voice, your personality, or your posts will not be compelling.

Personal business posts

Yes! I am down 19 pounds and 6 inches off my waistline since deciding to live a healthy life. I'm doing the happy dance over here. Be sure to include a smiling photo of yourself.

Weekly update posts

I love doing walk-throughs in houses. I did four this week for my real estate business. It always amazes me how the architecture changes in every home. Insert a picture or video of a house interior with great architecture.

Educational posts

Organic seems to be a hot topic. For suntan lotion to be considered organic, it must (insert your answer).

Ask your friends posts

Would anyone have an interest in receiving a sample? I've been using this mineral makeup for the last few months, and my skin feels fantastic. I've met a few hundred people already getting similar results.

Personal Business, Weekly, Educational, and Ask Your Friends posts are all useful variations of business posts.

Timing and frequency

Merely applying the 80/20 rule isn't enough. Factors like timing and frequency are equally important.

Timing

When possible, I post once in the morning, once in the afternoon, and once around 6 pm in my time zone. Sometimes, I'll post once for the entire day because the likes and comments continue to rise. At four in the morning one day, I did an inspirational post: a black-and-white selfie with words of how I felt at that moment. Throughout the day, people continued to like and comment on that reflective post. I believed it might make a difference in their lives, so I decided it would be the only post I made that day. By evening, the post had many likes and comments. People sent me private messages, telling me how the post inspired them at the start of their day.

Frequency

Obey the four-hour rule. I tend not to post within four hours of my previous post. Why? I notice fewer likes and comments on my posts when I post more often, and social media works against you when you post with high frequency. It's not in the best interest of social media sites to show all of your posts to your friends' at the expense of their other friends' posts. People want to see what all of their friends are doing, not just one friend who dominates social media.

On the flip side of that same theory, it's also essential to post at least once a day because not all of your friends see your posts all of the time.

Links

Inserting links into a post encourages people to click on whatever content you deem essential. Posting links are also like a one-way train ticket. People who follow the link are not likely to return to your post. Without likes or comments, you cannot be sure your friends are looking at your posts. Likes and comments give you a prime opportunity to continue communication. How can you build a relationship with your friends when your links encourage them to leave your post?

Links in personal posts

Instead of inserting a link to an article or source you believe has excellent content, become familiar with the article or source, mine the crucial pieces, and reflect on them inside a post. Encourage communication about the subject inside the comment section of your post instead of driving your friends to another website.

For example, let's say I read an article about success that resonated with me. Instead of posting a link to the article and sending my friends away to read the article, I took out pieces that were important to me and shared my thoughts about those pieces—what I learned and how it related to my life. It's no different from meeting a friend for coffee and saying, "Hey, I read this great tip about how to get the best airline deals." Would you then tell your friend, "You should pick up the same magazine and read all about it?" Heck no. You'd give them a tip, right then and there, then expound on how this nugget of information relates to your life. In turn, your friend would likely offer feedback from his or her life associated with the same topic. Social media is no different.

Links in business posts

Instead of inserting a link, which I assume would send your friends to your website or a landing page to give them more information about your business, why not choose one thing about your business that's important to you and post about it? Let your friends like and comment.

Then take the communication private with each friend. People are more likely to do business with you when you communicate directly with them. Driving them to a website discourages effective communication. Links in business posts send your friends away with a one-way ticket to Make-Your-Own-Decision Land, a place where you neither reside nor visit. Stay active in the process of your friend deciding to do business with you. Encourage friends to stay and like or comment.

The reset button

Hitting the reset button for 30 days may feel, at first, like treading backwards. In reality, you'll be taking a giant leap forward.

When I met Ben, he was posting more than 20% a week about business. Like everyone else, he did it for the right reasons. He thought that if he stayed in front of people about his business, they would do business with him in a shorter period.

After we communicated, he committed to me. Under no circumstance would he post more than 20% a week about his business. I asked him to spend the next 30 days only talking about his personal life since all of his friends were used to him talking about business all the time.

"Think of it as a reset button," I said.

He agreed.

After 30 days, Ben noticed a lot of his social media friends who had not communicated with him much in the past conversed with him a great deal more. This reset, alone, made him fall in love with social media. He said that even if his business did not grow, he was thankful that he was developing real friendships. Ben focused on the 20% rule for the 30 days following this reset period. Forty-five days later, Ben and ten of his 250-member distributor network had captured just over 60 new customers and many of these customers referring their friends to his business as well. Ben was ecstatic. He had never seen this type of growth before in such a short period.

Are you like Ben when I first met him? Don't be afraid to do a reset.

Responding to my friend's posts

Responding to friends' posts shows your friends you care about their lives. Dedicating a minimum of five minutes a day will go a long way for your business.

Like a friend's post when you do not have anything meaningful to say or your response is strictly an emotion that you feel. Consider adding emoticons based on the feeling you want to portray.

I like to pull out my phone and scroll throughout the day. It's easy to find a minute here and a minute there to do this activity. No sooner do I like a post that I see that same person liking or commenting on one of my posts. It sure beats the days that I had to call everyone on the phone to have the same type of communication.

Comment on a friend's post when you have something meaningful to say. Talk from the heart and be yourself. You will gain new friends from those who are reading the comments on your friend's post.

Most of my comments are less than five words long. You don't have to write a novel to create meaning. You need to speak from your heart. I also love to use stickers and gifs in place of words when I'm commenting. For example, I could write, I love this post. Thank you for sharing, or I can use the sticker of a giant smiley face where the eyes are replaced with hearts. More often than not, I tend to use the smiley face in place of words — me, being more emotional.

6 | The Four Cs

The Four Cs were created over a quarter of a century. This longevity gives you the absolute certainty for success if you apply the social media system to your business. This chapter is devoted to giving you the rich history and understanding of how the social media system was created for you.

The untold social media story

When I was living in Arizona, a friend of eleven years named Paul contacted me to join him as a consultant in a promising network marketing company. I kindly declined because I just finished building the largest social media agency in the state. My joy came from building companies—businesses of all types—too big success stories using social media.

Paul shared that the owner and co-founder of the company, Matt, used to be a million-dollar consultant with another company. This previous company had changed its compensation plan without warning, thus hurting every one of their consultants. Everyone's checks showed an immediate decrease.

As a result, Matt made a company-wide call. He asked any co-consultants whose earnings had gone down as a result of this changed compensation plan to contact him. For each person who approached him, he paid the difference in their checks until they were able to get their financial footing back.

Matt's selfless gesture made me want to meet this man.

Paul introduced me to the vice-president of marketing for the company—protocol before meeting the company owner. Surprisingly, the VP of marketing had also been a consultant in the same company for which I was a consultant 12 years prior—the same company where I was the company's top enroller and produced 40% of the top enrollers in the company because of social media.

Instant connection. I showed the VP of marketing our social media system. He immediately wanted to connect me with Matt. Matt and I spoke on a video call, and then he asked me if I could fly to Texas and visit the office.

When I landed, I had no expectations. I walked into a board room with ten people. We spent hours talking about where the company was and where they wanted to go. I loved their story. They wanted the best for everyone it seemed, and it was a great environment. Matt asked me if I would help them grow their company using social media. I kindly accepted the opportunity.

At the time, we were heading into December, one of the slowest times of the year in network marketing. I was starting the first of January with the company as a corporate executive, so Marianne, my wife, and I spent December testing our social media system with their product. By the end of December, we had moved more than $23,000 in product sales and built an excellent team of distributors. I knew then we had something we could work within social media. January was fun. New city. New life. New experiences. We got to work.

Here is the case study that documents what happened next. I'll show it to you in the original layout and structure as first written in 2014 without the use of the company or product names for confidential reasons.

Case Study: ███████ Social Media Strategy
Version 1.0: 4/28/2014
Presented by: Jim Lupkin

Company Profile

███████ Holdings, Inc., a network marketing company, offers wellness products targeting individuals and families. Products are sold

The company's principal products include:

- An all-in-one nutritional drink. It is a blend of whole food concentrates providing a source of nutrients, antioxidants, and vitamins
- Protein shakes designed to block carbohydrate absorption and leave you with a satisfied, full feeling
- An herbal and probiotic cleanse that helps detoxify the body and restore the digestive system to a healthy state
- A metabolism accelerator to burn calories, reduce the hunger, and block the absorption of the carbohydrates
- A weight management program that combines the products above to assist the consumer in losing weight or maintaining a 'healthier' weight

The company business model is network marketing. The business model compensates independent sales consultants for acquiring customers and building a sales organization of independent consultants, earning an override on their customers.

The business model is marketed by word of mouth, face to face and online. Independent sales consultants have an opportunity to earn money.

Overview

In 2012, the company Facebook business page had four million impressions, reached 817,900k people, generated 54,383 stories, and had 4,300 likes. Total revenue in 2012 was $12m.

Based on progress from 2012 figures:

- Impressions increased– 725%
- Reach increased– 572%
- New fans increased– 705%
- Stories increased– 653%

Business definitions: Impressions and Reach is one way of showing brand value. The more people who see the brand, the more valuable the company becomes in the market. New fans mean the company's customer retention and advocacy are getting stronger. Stories indicate the number of prospects that could have ordered the products or became a consultant.

Facebook definitions: Impressions are the total number of times any Facebook user has seen content from the company. Reach is the number of unique people who saw content associated with the company. Fans are people who know the company's page and click "like." A story on Facebook is created when a user likes your page, posts to the company's wall, answers a question, RSVP's to one of the company's events, mentions the company's page, photo tags the company's page, checks in, or likes, comments, or shares one of the company's page posts.

Problem:

The company wanted to grow its social media presence while increasing in three key performance areas of the business:

- Strengthen customer and consultant base
- Enrich the consultant culture
- Convert sales and increase revenue

Solution:

The following strategies were used to achieve the desired outcomes in the three key performance areas:

- Redeveloped the company's Facebook Business Page: The page included new content and design. Examples of new material included but were not limited to, contests, product testimonials, and product ingredients. The page was launched in January 2013. In 2013, a brief marketing campaign was initiated with a total of $17,500 and $3,000 a month spent in 2014 to support the consultants in building influence with their friends on Facebook.

- Consultant Social Media Training Program: A step-by-step action plan teaching existing consultants on how to generate new customers and consultants on Facebook. The training program was launched in February 2013.

- Facebook Groups: A way to support customers and consultants 24/7. Also, consultants had access to corporate, field leadership, ongoing social media training, and others who were also consultants.

Results:

	Year 2012	Year 2013	* 2014
Impressions	4 million	21.2 million	47.2 million
Reach	817,900	2.7 million	11.2 million
New Fans/Likes	4,300	24,000	42,400
Stories Created	54,383	310,324	396,400
Revenue	$11 million	$63 million	N/A

*2014: 1st quarter data is actual. Annual data
is estimated based on an annualized trend

Strengthening the customer and consultant base was achieved through social engagement using Facebook. People felt a sense of support when purchasing the product for its promoted health benefits and when taking on the new challenge of building a business. Because customers and consultants experienced product and business support in a social environment, they asked questions, talked to others sampling the product or growing the business for the first time, and found support regarding concerns or questions they had.

New Consultant: Cheri
Cheri says, "Jodi posted on Facebook about
the product, and it interested us.
We signed up with a builder's pack.
The best $500 we ever spent!"

The consultant culture became more enriched because of the newly developed support systems and social media training program. The most common reason for failure in network marketing is due to inaction by the freshly appointed consultant, and inaction often occurs because of a lack of skills or experience in running a network marketing business. Often the allure of working from home and the freedoms that entail are inspiring but is too soon met with the reality of not having the proper skill set to perform the duties of running a network marketing business. Through proper education, training, and support, failure can be significantly alleviated, which creates a stronger and happier consultant. It also keeps a consultant involved longer with the company.

New Consultant: Krista
Krista says, "I Facebook-creeped my friend
Tiffany for six months before joining.
My family's health has done a 180 since!
Yay for Facebook!"

Converted sales and increased revenue occurred when attendance to the consultant-led marketing events known as "Challenge Parties" significantly increased through proper training in social media marketing. With new skill sets in social media promotion, consultants were able to effectively announce the events and drive traffic to registrations for upcoming "Challenge Parties." This led to an increase in sales.

New Consultant: Debbie

Debbie says, "I have a friend on Facebook that kept posting about the product. Well, I gave in and went to one of those Challenge Parties. I don't know where I would be without these products. I am now a consultant."

Even though there was a dramatic uplift in the number of prospects, advocacy, brand value, and customer retention, there were also sales generated.

To understand the impact on sales, I posted a question on the company's Facebook business page. I asked, "Before becoming a customer or consultant did a friend talk to you on Facebook about the company or did you do research on the products through Facebook?" The number of people who answered these two questions was 3,946.

An astounding 2094 participants answered yes to both questions.

Services used to create case study:

- Sprout Social, a preferred partner of Facebook, provided all the data
- Facebook was the only social media platform used
- Facebook ads were used to support consultants in building influence with friends
- Video and Facebook Groups delivered consultant social media training
- Additional training was provided by webinar, live events, and one-on-one

Questions:

Additional questions or comments about this case study may be directed to:
Jim Lupkin, Social Media Director for the company.
https://www.facebook.com/jimlupkin

Not a day goes by that I don't remember this company. This case study happened at a time when businesses were starting to figure out social media, and I have been doing it for 19 years. That year, according to annual sales by Direct Selling News Magazine and validated by Facebook's preferred third-party partner, BrandWatch, the company became the most engaged network marketing company on Facebook out of the top 100 network marketing companies. While many marketers have a strong understanding of paid advertising on Facebook today, very few, if any, know how to harness the power of word of mouth.

Working on this project created dozens of genuine friendships that I still have today. I owe the company's renewed social media success to a group of passionate consultants and to owners committed to building their company.

Social media opened my mind to worlds I never knew existed, from having access to world-class coaches to learning from influential mentors, and, most importantly, meeting the love of my life who is now my wife, Marianne.

Social media is so much more than business to me. It's life.

Refining the four cs over 25 years

My social media experience and research started decades ago. I was a desperate 18-year-old kid who had many ideas on success but could find no one to listen. Inside a clunky, big, grey box called a desktop computer, I found an audience and a trajectory.

In October 1995, as a senior in high school, I became an independent contractor for a company called ACN. ACN marketed telecommunication services, like long distance phone service and pagers. Over four years, I recruited 40 independent contractors, which turned into a team of 800 independent contractors capturing more than 3,000 customers in the US. I accomplished all of this by employing some of the earliest forms of social media.

After our school's librarian taught a handful of students, myself included, how to use the computer, I stumbled upon AOL message boards and eventually Yahoo Chat groups.

I happened upon a message board called "small business." No one judged me. Even though I was an 18-year-old kid living in a Pennsylvania coal town of 13,000 people, everyone listened. I started to enroll customers and independent contractors into ACN. It was amazing.

While there weren't as many people online in the 1990s as there are today, I still connected with an average of 30 new people each week. Up to this point, hardly anyone would listen to me. The moment they realized my age, that I was still in high school, they concluded that I didn't have enough life experience to be successful in business of any kind.

In 2001, I had the unique opportunity to work with one of the best mentors I ever had: Mark Yarnell. As a distributor in network marketing, Mark developed an international organization of more than 300,000 distributors in 21 countries. He was the only person from network marketing to serve as Contributing Editor to Success Magazine, and he and Dr. Charles King of Harvard University co-created the first certification course in network marketing taught at the University of Illinois, Chicago from 1993-2011. He touched the lives of millions and is known for his bestselling book Your First Year in Network Marketing.

Mark rapidly expanded my knowledge of network marketing and direct sales and with my ability to never run out of people to talk to using social media. I enrolled 600 distributors for a company called Legacy for Life in only two years. Even more thrilling, 40% of the top distributors based on personal production were on my team. I coached these distributors how, where, and when to use the elements of social media as they built businesses.

Mark influenced me to push forward with social media when he said, "We aren't ready yet for this computer thing. However, one day, when someone can figure out how to build real relationships online the way we do face to face, that company will build the largest network marketing company in the world."

I took my social media skills and co-founded a small business in the software space. Using social media, primarily MySpace, we generated more than 1,200 clients. Our jobs ranged from simple $500 flash presentations, $25,000 sophisticated websites, and $40,000 enterprise software clients throughout Asia to wholesale work with existing web companies in the US averaging $150,000 in sales over six months.

And yes, even the more significant sales came because of relationships created through social media.

Next, my team and I built a social network to compete against Facebook and MySpace. It was a grueling nine months of writing code and designing hundreds of web pages with 18 developers and four designers. Our website, Ojeez, was the 17,000th most visited website in the world out of 85 million, according to its Alexa rating (Alexa is a website that has ranked the most popular sites on the web since 1996). Ojeez was also nominated for the 2008 Emerging Technology List by Alwayson-Network.

Towards the end of 2008, I attended the first social media event happening in the US in Denver, Colorado. It took me 13 years to realize what I was doing online had a name. The speaker at the event called it "social media." I just saw it as making new friends online then asking those friends to do business with me. At the end of the event, hundreds of people were still confused because the speaker did not teach how to grow a business using social media. We decided to start a social media agency called WeBuildYourSocialMedia (WBYSM), later renamed to Summa Social, to help independent contractors, small businesses, brands, and companies who were confused. We taught businesses how to build relationships on social media sites that generated sales.

Within our first year, we helped 100+ small businesses with their social media management, campaigns, and content creation and trained over 1,000 businesses through seminars. By year two, we had helped over 250 small businesses and trained over 5,000 businesses, and by year three we had assisted more than 400 small businesses and taught 18,000 businesses. In our second year, we built software to manage social media content, post scheduling, and marketing to support 8,000 businesses. Two of our most important projects were co-managing 4,000 apartment complexes on Facebook with our ForRent.com partnership and working with Dr. Mikel Harry, co-creator of the world-renowned Six Sigma. The Six Sigma system is used by 87 of the Fortune 100 companies in the United States, like American Express, Ford, General Electric, and the big e-commerce company of our time, Amazon, and by two-thirds of the Fortune 500 companies. Six Sigma helps companies maximize their efficiency and increase profit.

Dr. Mikel Harry's friendship opened my eyes to the importance of sequence, timing, and process when developing simple systems that yield maximum success.

You'll find Six Sigma's philosophy throughout my social media system.

In October 2012, my wife, Marianne, relocated to Arizona. She wanted to be an entrepreneur without needing to raise much money, open an office, or hire employees and work part-time because she had to travel every other month for a week to Pennsylvania for the Airforce National Guard. She joined a network marketing company called ViSalus, which markets "Body by VI Challenge," a platform for weight loss and fitness results. Her team did $13,000 in product sales within 45 days by using social media. Due to her regimented military commitment and because we were life partners, I had a unique opportunity to teach her around the clock while at the same time coming up with a simplified version of my social media system.

A few months later, and for personal reasons, she joined a new company called Zurvita. At Zurvita, her team produced $23,000 in product sales during the first 30 days by using social media. She accomplished this feat with a new group of distributors, using the new simplified version of my social media system, and during one of the slowest times of the year for network marketing companies—December.

Zurvita also offered me the opportunity to work on the corporate side, running social media company-wide. Using Facebook and Challenge Parties, along with hardworking distributors and a committed corporate team, Zurvita grew by $70 million in company sales in just 16 months.

My time at Zurvita sparked the inspiration to write my first book, Network Marketing for Facebook, which became an Amazon #1 best-seller.

Social media is always updating, changing, and expanding. So, too, are the lives and demands of those who use it daily to interact with friends and for business. My inspiration to develop a system came from the blessing of being friends with the co-creator of Six Sigma, Dr. Mikel Harry. Marianne and I worked with more than 750 businesses over four months with dozens of different products and services in 30 countries. We developed our social media system you are reading about in this book. We shared it with Dr. Mikel Harry for his review and the unthinkable happened. He told us he wanted to endorse the social media system. According to his research and understanding, our social media system is the only proven system in the world to help businesses grow using word of mouth on social media the right way. He believed our system could change the world of business the same way Six Sigma had.

It took a bit more time after that for us to solidify our research, experience, and the expression of our social media system, but now it's ready for you. During this time, I was also appointed as the Executive Director of the Social Networking Association (formerly known as MLMIA), a 33-year-old association created to help direct sales and network marketing companies, distributors and support companies be successful around the world.

I wish this social media epiphany had happened overnight. I'd have more hair today. However, seeing the early versions of social media has provided me a better sense of what's going to survive in the future. The past ten years have mainstreamed the acceptance of social media as a job, and I've experienced nothing but success. I'm giving you the keys to a door it took me more than two decades to unlock so you can meet with success right away.

The four cs timing, sequence, and process

I've distilled my system into four key components. I call them the Four Cs: community, conversation, connection, and communication. Together, these four create a simple but powerful social media system.

- Community: Create a 24-hour support network to inspire people to do business with you today by applying social proof
- Conversation: Learn the art of building real relationships and influence around your business with real people using one-on-one and group chats
- Connection: Discover how to never run out of people to talk to for your business by meeting people who like and trust you
- Communication: Build a list of people who want to do business with you in the future since most people will not do business with you today

Working the four cs together

Some people know how to connect with others on social media, while some only understand parts of a conversation. Some people who can't build real relationships through conversations or connecting with others are fabulous at follow up or creating communities. If you learn how to use all four components, you will be able to grow your business systematically and progressively. Like an orchestra, every instrument will play harmoniously together to create a masterpiece. It's about innovation. It's about developing the proper sequence, timing, and process to make the entire social media ecosystem work for you.

So remember, social media works, if you work it.

Made in the USA
Lexington, KY
27 May 2019